COMING TO AWE,

Expressing Identity

PART 3: EXPRESSION

LOWELL ROUTLEY, PH.D.

www.xulonpress.com

ACKNOWLEDGEMENTS

COMING TO AWE, EXPRESSING IDENTITY
Author: Lowell Routley, Ph.D.
Manuscript Editor: Terry Routley, B.A.
Instructional Design Editor: Kris Anderson, M.Div.
Graphics Editor: Glory Hougham, B.A.
Focus Editor: Wil Anderson, D.Min.
Xulon Publishing Team

Enough gratitude can never be expressed for these who have worked patiently with my Core desire to communicate these principles and thereby teach others how to live an identity-driven life.

I thank Terry, my wonderful wife, whose Core traits are grace, love, acceptance, and wisdom that reflects the Spirit of God in who she is. Her years in publishing made her the perfect editor. She found the words I needed for clarity.

Glory, a coworker in a number of spiritual endeavors, manifests Core traits of patience, intuition, creativity, and encouragement that challenged me to excellence, but just do it--write!

Kris uses his gifts to make any learning experience helpful for students. His Core desire is for people to learn the Word of God and apply it personally in day-to-day life. Kris is the third generation of Andersons; I thank God for bringing them into my life.

Wil, the grandfather of the Andersons, with his wife Nan raised an extended family who each in his or her Core being values a personal relationship with the Creator and each seeks to introduce others to a personal knowledge of Christ. Wil from his pastor's heart with his Core traits of thoughtfulness, faithfulness, attention, and account-ability reflects a life of Core integrity. His many years of service to the Gospel of Christ in missions, pastoral ministry, training, and counseling impacted many lives. Wil kept me focused with the simple question, "Where is the Awe?" I would go back to writing. When I finally heard him say, "Now that brought me to Awe," I knew the message was being expressed.

I am also grateful to Xulon, who helped as an organization ded-icated to Christian publishing and to their publishing team whose expertise helped to put the manuscript in print and onto bookshelves for purchase.

I hope that you also will see the awesome truth of who you are because Creator God planned for you before the foundation of the world to experience a full and abundant life. May you catch the awe, be transformed, and share the awe with others.

PREFACE

The Culmination of a Dream

During the early years of my counseling practice, I noticed how Christians struggled to understand who they were, how they were to act, and how they were to feel. The questions posed in counseling were about what was sinful and what was natural human experience. One example was the belief that emotional turmoil was proof of sin in the believer's life. Emotions were not understood. Anyone showing emotional distress was judged as lacking faith.

If someone grieved six months after the loss of a loved one, he or she may have been seen as wallowing in self-pity. Another individual might have expressed anxiety about a relationship, a job, or a decision to be made. After a time, many faith communities showed impatience because they did not know how to support. Community has an unspoken agenda for how long a person's struggle should last. To feel anxious or afraid was seen as a lack of faith.

What I would share is how the Creator expressed a range of emotions toward humanity--from anger at humanity's behavior to love for those who followed Him. With His image as the template for humanity, emotion would be a natural feature to find. While this topic comes up less in my last decade of counseling, the confusion about emotions is still there.

Relational problems within families and among friends may be attributed to one person lacking submission to spiritual authority. The conflict may arise from disagreement as to who is the spiritual authority or that the person of perceived authority is wrong about what the real problem is. Role confusion, power and control issues, or past woundedness may result in failed relationships. Christians with a rigid stance against divorce reject the one who files for divorce and sees him or her as the sinner. When the faith community gathers around the one objecting to the divorce, it is assumed that the community is supporting the wronged person when in reality they may be supporting the wrong person. Remember that the Relational identity does not always represent the Core truth.

Christians like to solve problems in a simple manner by finding the spiritual recipe for how to handle difficult emotions or relationships. Many good books are available for individuals and communities of faith that provide insights and recommendations for problem solving. However, humanity in general likes quick fixes. That human trait is related to the curse from Adam's sin—hard work would be required outside of Eden. So humanity seeks to make any work easier by passing the responsibility to another or avoiding the work altogether. Jesus told the disciples that change required much intention and prayer. He encouraged His followers not to lose heart because, like the disciples, you and I are overcomers through Him.

The trend of Christians being warned to not seek any counselor including one that is a Christian trained in secular behavioral science is slowly changing. Psychology was viewed as dangerous, seducing Christians away from using faith and God's word to solve problems. Some Christian leaders would tell parishioners that taking psychotropic medication showed lack of faith. Some said troubles were caused by spiritual oppression from demonic influence in a believer's life. A person was told to stop taking the medication and pray harder. The side effects of going off medication cold turkey are dangerous possibly leading to extended hospitalizations or suicides. These were often deeply wounded people with such deep shame that they did not feel safe to tell their stories.

One pastor told a couple who had seen me for three years to stop seeing me and come to him. He had been trained in Biblical pastoral counseling at seminary and he would help them in six to twelve weeks. They sought his counsel faithfully. The pastor became overwhelmed, frustrated, and dismissed them after ten weeks. His parting words were that they were sinful, rebellious, and unrepentant.

Ironically, the husband was a wealthy professional who was one of the largest contributors to Christian ministries, including that church. This philosophy of counseling is still promoted by some. After a few weeks without signs of change that the pastor determined necessary, he would write off the hurting person, convincing himself that if the person really wanted to, he or she would change.

Church leaders did not know that a parallel was happening in the secular world. Brief therapy and employee assistance programs were seen as the solution to expensive mental health care insurance and treatment. When people did not improve, they were labeled resistant and put on strong medications, reinforcing the belief for those believers who heard from church this was lack of faith. The response of some secular mental health professionals was to tell the person that religion was causing their problems, so put away their Bible and stop going to church. Freud's interpretation was that Calvinistic guilt clashed with the Victorian mindset of prudishness. If people just did what felt good and not guilt themselves, there would be relief.

The wounded, hurting person was let down on two fronts and left without recourse. Medication regimes were constantly being tweaked to maintain moods and functioning. Managed mental health care allowed six to twelve 45-minute visits per year as adequate for talk therapy. The suffering individual would attend church and to avoid guilt and social rejection did not share their pain with anyone. Knowing of this dilemma, I hoped that I could make a measurable difference in many people's lives. Each time I repeated certain topics, I would have three thoughts: if only I had the ability to write; if I just wrote this out, many more could benefit; and lastly, given my caseload, if only I had the time to write.

The reality was I could see one person at a time with whom I could sit, listen to, understand, provide options to bring relief, and assure that person of the loving kindness of our Creator. He took on human flesh, lived within His creation without sin, and became our healer. To know that we are heard, that we are not alone, that another can relate to our struggle was the message I shared with many over these years. That truth transformed suffering, healed wounds, and provided comfort for hundreds of people who shared their suffering with me. A significant part of that message was that our Creator endowed each of us with a unique Core identity. Yet the people with whom we were raised shaped our social identity, our Relational self.

I always wanted to write out what I found in the practical teachings about Jesus Christ from Scripture. I often shared my desire to write out something on the emotions that Jesus displayed as evidence of His humanity. Ironically, Jesus was never seen by His Father as sinful because of the emotions He expressed. He lived His life from His Core identity and showed what the Creator intended for humanity before sin entered the picture. All His behavior, speech, and character were pure. Consider how Jesus expressed emotion.

He expressed anger when overthrowing the kiosks in the Temple courtyard. He scattered the unfit animals being sold as an acceptable sacrifice in the Temple. He used a whip to drive out the bankers whose currency exchange rates cheated pilgrims coming to worship. All this because He was angry with people who flagrantly defiled the place sanctified for prayer and worship of Jehovah, Israel's God.

He displayed deep grief, ululating loudly, pounding on His chest, and publicly shedding tears over the death of His friend, Lazarus. He shocked His friends gathered at the grave four days after Lazarus was buried. All the onlookers saw by His expression that His grief was genuine. The manner in which Jesus displayed His grief was proof of the depth of His love for Lazarus.

The Garden of Gethsemane was where Jesus encountered depression as any human being would. His disciples were oblivious to His suffering of which they were a part. Though He had just told them he faced betrayal, abandonment, and death at the Passover meal, they did not comprehend. The eleven disciples left Him alone in His anguish as He prayed to His Father. Depression comes from being alone and rejected as He was in His suffering while the disciples slept. Even His father would turn from Him.

Depression comes from being trapped. Jesus prayed in His humanity to be freed from what He was about to face. His pleas for His Father's deliverance from what He knew lay ahead were heart breaking. Yet He submitted to the Father's will. No angel would stay the Father's hand as was done for Abraham and Isaac. He obediently fulfilled His Father's will, drank the bitter cup, and died separated from His Father.

Depression also grows out of feelings of guilt and shame for sins committed. Jesus knew He would bear our sin and feel our guilt and shame, He who had never sinned. How horrific it must have been for Him to witness evil in this world during His lifetime. How indescribably awful it must have been for Him, pure and innocent, to be covered by every sin of every individual from Adam and Eve to the end of time. One person's struggle with all his shame and guilt is barely survivable. Jesus Christ had the burden of all humanity's sin laid on Him.

Depression is provoked by injustice. Jesus Christ, the righteous one, died in our place, the just for the unjust, to bring us to God. Oh, what Jesus Christ endured on the Cross for you and me! He expressed His anger as His Father shunned Him because the Holy Father does not look on sin. He could not look at His own Son because all He would see was your sin and mine. Nevertheless, Jesus Christ showed no bitterness, but cried out with compassion that the Father would forgive us. What I just wrote was what I hoped to write some day about the emotions of Jesus. Jesus, fully God and fully human, shows us that emotion itself is not sin. Rather, the choices a human being makes and the actions that result fit James' operational definition of sin: Remember, it is sin to know what you ought to do and then not do it. James 4:17 NLT

I have written this series *Coming to Awe, Finding Identity* as a compilation of my years of counseling experience and from my personal relationship with my Creator. I pray that as you read these ideas you may be redeemed, transformed, and stirred to express you joy and gratitude for our amazing Creator. I hope that you come to know His loving kindness in a deep, personal way on a daily basis. I trust that you will come to know your Core being and express daily praise for His great love. May you become one to introduce others to the Creator who gave them existence, to experience His amazing love, and to express through service and worship the praise He is due. Please read on to learn how your Core expression of service and worship is the ultimate purpose of humanity, the culmination of the Creator's design.

TABLE OF CONTENTS

Section 3.1: Let all that I am, praise the Lord

"Let all that I am praise the Lord; with my whole heart, I will praise his holy name. Let all that I am praise the Lord; may I never forget the good things he does for me." (Psalm 103:1-2 NLT)

[This series, *Coming to Awe, Finding Identity,* of which this is the third volume, seeks to acquaint the reader with what it means to be created in the image of God. None of what is written regarding these concepts intends to neither lessen our Creator nor elevate humanity. To the contrary, I become awestruck by the Creator's plan, design, and fulfillment.

Each of the three volumes has a central theme regarding identity that reflects an aspect of our Creator's image manifest in humanity. **Origin**—Our Core identity has existence and identity endowed by our Creator from conception. **Influence**—Our Relational identity, shaped by life experiences, results in a false self that usurps our Core identity. **Integrity**—Our Core identity restored, seeks to honor the Creator by expressing praise and gratitude with our whole being.

My hope is that what you learn from this series will provoke you to live from your Core being. In this final book, we will explore what it means to express from our Core identity consistent with the Creator's design. This introductory chapter sets the stage for how the Creator designed us to express from our Core being. My hope is that you become amazed by the beauty of His design and see it actively at work in your daily expression from your Core being.]

Chapter 1

EXPRESSING CORE FAITH

Through the Lens

My daughter Paula took a class in photography in high school that required an investment in a good camera, a Canon Rebel single lens reflex with a 300-millimeter zoom lens. After high school, Paula's interests changed and the camera became mine. I replaced the camera with a digital Canon Rebel XS that was compatible with the original lens. The mechanical eye had the ability to focus on and capture many images of people, places, and things from a distance. I love capturing the expressions on people's faces when they are in their Core identity, and totally unaware of being observed.

The cover images of the three books are the same child with different facial expressions. The images were moments with my grandson, Micah. He was unaware that Papa was taking his picture, so the expressions naturally show the three states of Core identity—existence (being in the moment without judgment), experience (reacting to the moment in disbelief, surprise, or confusion), and expression (using the moment to share the feelings of joy with songful praise).

To the children that I hold dear, I am known as "Papa." When I found these images, I asked permission of my grandson Micah, his sister Lydia, and brothers Noah and Josiah, and their parents to use pictures and stories to illustrate the principles in this series. I am grateful to each and rejoice in who each is in that precious Core identity endowed by the Creator.

Lydia, an avid sportsperson, expresses her Core values and challenges her peers to work together and play fair. Lydia has her dad's passion about athletics. Both Lydia and Micah participate in a children's worship choir expressing praise to the Creator from their Core being. Micah expresses his Core gifts of creativity and imagination even when he is on his own as the cover images show. Noah explores the world of ideas and possibilities often surprising others with his unique observations. He catches his mom off guard with questions like, "Mom. Is debate class about arguing? If it is, I want to take it." Noah's imagination awakens others to see things in life from a different perspective. Little Joe, eager to go school, began to memorize and quote Bible verses. You know when he is done because he puts emphasis on the Biblical reference of book, chapter, and verse so anyone who listens will know where to find it in God's word. He can explain its meaning to any who ask.

The cover images of Micah were captured through that 300-millimeter zoom lens without his knowledge of being watched. Over the years, that lens has been my window to observe people being in the moment in their Core identity. I have done photo journals of weddings for close friends. The bride and groom focus on one another losing sight of the fact that others are watching. In their love for each other, they have private moments when they do not notice others' presence. Those Core moments captured during the ceremony and at the reception are taken and given as a present to remind the couple of their first love.

Child-like Faith

"You have taught children and infants to tell of your strength, silencing your enemies and all who oppose you." (Psalm 8:2 NLT)

"Do you hear what these children are saying? ...Jesus replied. Haven't you ever read the Scriptures? For they say, 'You have

taught children and infants to give you praise.'" (Matthew
21:16 NLT)

I believe that the Creator intended children to remind adults of
the Creator's desire. He gave children the ability to use simple words
and actions to proclaim profound truth. How expressive the Creator
designed children to be. His intent was that the Core identity He
endowed in each child would express praise and bring adults back
to their own Core being to seek the kingdom of God.

The Pharisees were among the most learned men of the world
at the time of Jesus. When affronted by the words of the children
who were singing God's praises, the Pharisees expected Jesus to
silence them. Instead, Jesus responded to the Pharisees by reminding
them of a phrase from Psalm 8 that they knew well. The truth of the
phrase was that the Creator taught children to speak of His character
with words that could silence any opposition. In present day situations, any adult who screams at a happy, singing child to silence
her betrays his own hostility toward the truth and the wisdom of the
child's expression. The Creator speaks truth through the natural innocence and simple understanding of a child because no ingrained life
experiences color the child's expression. A child accepts truth with
simple faith.

One day, the crowd around Jesus was parents bringing their children, even babies, so that He would bless them by His touch and heal
their ills. The disciples scolded the parents for bothering Jesus with
the children. The story shows the cultural mindset of the day reflected
in the disciples' attitudes that mimics the American culture of the
1930s through the 1970s—"children should be seen and not heard."
Jesus intentionally invites the children to walk past the adults and
approach Him. I can imagine one nine-year-old child walking past
James with a big grin on her face. As an eight-year-old boy passes
Peter to go to Jesus, he looks at Peter and subtly sticks out his tongue.
Children knew in their Core being they were welcome.

With the children gathered round, Jesus looked up to see adults
surprised that Jesus gave children priority over them. Jesus used the
moment to teach truth to the adults. He told the adults that the only
way for them to receive the kingdom of God was to have the simple

faith of a child. Those children standing with Jesus accepted what He said. A child in his or her Core being knew Jesus was the Creator and the Messiah. These children had heard their parents speak of the God of Israel who had rescued them from Egypt and now had brought them home to the Promised Land from another captivity.

The adults present that day, even the disciples who intimately knew Jesus, were under the influence of their Relational self responding as they had been socialized and acculturated. Scripture shows teachable moments like these resulted in the disciples following Jesus more fully from their Core being. Not long after this event, Jesus asked the disciples if they would leave Him as other followers were. Peter answered Jesus, speaking for all twelve disciples, "Lord, to whom would we go? You have the words that give eternal life. We believe, and we know you are the Holy One of God." (John 6:68 NLT)

Jesus knew one disciple present among the twelve hid behind Peter's words in feigned faith. Judas focused on the material world. Judas was onboard for the socio-political cause. Jesus was to lead the rebellion that reestablished the sovereign state of Israel free from Roman rule. Governed totally by his Relational self, Judas realized when the cause was lost. Judas did not listen to his Core being where child-like faith resides. His focus was strictly on the external world and his Relational self did not want to be party to a lost cause. When Judas realized that Jesus spoke the truth of His death and that He would not become king, Judas turned Jesus over to the Sanhedrin and distanced himself from the cause. Judas did not have the faith of the child needed to embrace the kingdom of God.

Identity Assessment Exercise

"Today you are You, that is truer than true. There is no one alive who is Youer than You." Dr. Seuss[1]

The following exercise was introduced in volume one, chapter two. Please retake this expanded assessment. Keep in mind to answer based on an overview of your life or especially the past ten years. Make your answers descriptive of how you see yourself for who you really are, not as how you wish you were or how you wish to be seen by others. This simple exercise is the starting point to under-stand Core and Relational identities for the *Coming to Awe, Finding Identity* series.

✍ *Journal Time—Assessment of Core and Relational identity*

Print out six copies of this form with your personal information filled in at the top of the form. Complete the first copy as your own assessment. Give a copy of this form to five people who know you in different areas of life: like close family, extended family, colleague from work, friend from church, and your best friend, or your spouse. Ask them to complete the form as how they would think you would answer the questions.

Identity Assessment

Full birth name: _____

First Name / Middle Name / Last Name

Date of birth: _____ Current age: _____

Month / Day / Year

Five positive adjectives, like strengths or qualities that you believe best describes the kind of person you have been as an adult:

1.
2.
3.
4.
5.

Three personal values that you hold strongly in spite of what others might think:

1.
2.
3.

Five nouns that describe your job, social roles, hobbies, interests, and so on:

1.
2.
3.
4.
5.

Three people or settings that influence you in a healthy or positive way:

1.
2.
3.

Three people or settings that influence you in an unhealthy or negative way:

1.
2.
3.

✍ *Journal Time Ends — Assessment of Core and Relational identity*

What is the difference between Core identity and Relational identity? The first two lists above describe your Core identity and the last three lists describe your Relational identity. The purpose of this information is to provide you with the means to sort out who you really are from who others expect you to be.

This is a means to understand your Core identity and to differentiate it from your Relational identity, to take any needed steps for emotional health, and/or to grow from your Core identity into the identity the Creator intended for you. What you learn through this exercise has two benefits. If others define you, other than who the Creator intended you to be, you can seek relationships that will support your Core traits. If you wonder about how well you please your Creator, you can find ways to listen within your being to the Holy Spirit for wisdom, direction, encouragement, and strength.

Recognizing Core Identity — the Genuine Self

Core identity typically is associated to your birth name and your date of birth. The majority of people identify with their first and middle name being who they are. Your birth certificate proves your identity with the names of your parents and sometimes the grandparents' names, the doctor who delivered you, the hospital, home address, the date and time of birth, your birth weight, and your full name. Technically, your nickname or a shortened version of your name represents your Relational identity. The name Robert William Smith signifies Core identity. "Robert" might be accepted by or responded to by your Core as its name. However, Bob, Bobby, Rob, Smithy, Will, or any other derivation is associated to the Relational identity. That nickname is what others call you from the different social contexts of your life.

Why do we use adjectives to identify Core identity? An adjective is a word that describes a person, place, or thing. "Core identity" refers to you, the person who dwells inside of the physical you. You can think of the term Core identity as a placeholder for your birth name. Adjectives represent the best way to describe yourself with words that fit how you see yourself as a person. Adjectives have a feeling connection to who you are. They speak to personality and character. I like the British definition of adjective because of its deeper meaning; "an adjective is 'a word that *imputes* a characteristic.'"[2]

Based on William James' observation that "I" am the subject of my life,[3] our Core identity participates in what we find meaningful from within our spirit. In your heart of hearts, you know yourself for these <u>characteristics</u> and <u>values</u>; you expect others to recognize you by these characteristics. Your Core self has a felt-sense of these traits by looking inward to your mind and spirit. Some describe that knowledge as feeling natural and right. Please keep in mind that Core identity, Core being, and Core self are synonymous and are used interchangeably in this book.

Recognizing Relational Identity—The Identity Thief

Relational identity is how our social environment sees and knows us based on our interactions with them. Often these relationships use nicknames in speaking to or about us. When our relationships dictate who we are to be, our Relational identity must please, comply with, or control the perceptions of others. From infancy, parents begin to instruct the child in the principles and rules of socially acceptable behavior—when to eat, when to sleep, how to play, what emotions to display, and how to speak. These are some of the ways the child may be socialized into what parents determine is an acceptable human being.

Some parents look to guide the natural qualities of the child's Core identity, knowing that the unique Core identity will eventually emerge and take charge in its life. Other parents see the child as either an ignorant blank slate or a potential social misfit that must be conditioned to live by a rigid set of social rules. Socialization of such a nature wants to assure the child's behavior will not reflect badly on the parents. To prevent embarrassment, the parents protect their image by establishing a defined Relational identity that the child must display to avoid punishment. Those parents see the child as their possession to shape as they see fit. Traumatic socialization does not eradicate the Core identity; rather it constricts its emergence based on how strongly the Relational self was reinforced. Never the less, genuine identity is still there within the person and may manifest briefly during times of safety.

The Relational identity is driven by social emotions, especially fear, hurt, shame and guilt, or anger. The experiences of the Relational self are the memories that remind the child that being genuine is unsafe, even dangerous. The Relational self is externally defined and is driven to win social approval. The attention required to remain vigilant for the sake of safety creates a high state of ongoing stress for the individual. In our assessment exercise, the last three lists represent those actions and activities that you pursue from your Relational identity. These social behaviors may be how you might express your Core identity or may be how you might allow others to define you. Your Relational identity can undermine your Core identity if you seek to please, conform, or control the perceptions of others. The degree to which that happens reflects on how much you allow your adult self to be defined by others. When you allow yourself to be defined by others, they steal your true sense of identity.

Examples of two directions follow. One person may reflect that she always knew how much her identity traits and values were the foundation for her decisions. Another responds that he also knew these traits and values to be important and wanted them to guide his sense of self. To his chagrin, he admitted that he rarely followed his heart. His fear of rejection by or disapproval from others prevented him from living from his Core being. Another might encounter such terror from being other than what people expect that they have no sense of a clear Core identity.

Their Relational identity exists in the survival mindset of a chameleon, always changing to blend into the immediate environment. These people have wonderful qualities that others can see. However, because they learn to live with hypervigilance for self-protection, the external focus is all they consciously know. The flux of change from one identity to another is so rapid, they have no time to listen to their mind and heart.

When humanity became alienated from the Creator through Adam's sin, men still yearned to find something they sensed missing. Without knowledge of what had been lost, the Core identity of every individual remains unsettled until he or she acknowledges the Creator.

Despair and hopelessness can bring the Core self forward past the Relational self making it possible to seek and hear the Creator, experience the message of redemption, and break free of the shame that imprisons the Core identity.

Reclaiming Core Integrity

To encounter the Creator and experience His love and grace results in overwhelming awe. Even before we were born, He knew and loved us. Any who said to you that you were unlovable had no concept of the great love that our Creator has for us even when we are unlovable. In that moment of coming to truth and accepting it, we as human beings realize there is Someone greater than we are. We observed behind the events with mouth agape. The Creator in whose likeness we were formed is that Someone.

The Creator as a conscious being knows you and me in our Core being because, whether we know of Him or not, He gave us life and identity. Identity is not contingent on acceptance of the Creator; He bestowed identity as part of His creatorial design. Writings over the millennia of human existence express the majestic nature of an encounter with our Creator. The best resource for these expressions to me personally is found in Holy Scripture. A few examples that put into words Core expressions of wonder at our amazing Creator are found in these psalms.

> **He attends to the least**—"When I look at the night sky and see the work of your fingers—the moon and the stars you set in place—what are mere mortals that you should think about them, human beings that you should care for them? (Psalms 8:3-4 NLT)

> **All creation lauds Him**—"The heavens proclaim the glory of God. The skies display his craftsmanship. Day after day they continue to speak; night after night they make him known. They speak without a sound or word; their voice is never heard. Yet their message has gone throughout the earth, and their words to all the world." (Psalm 19:1-4 NLT)

Creation mimics His power—"But mightier than the violent raging of the seas, mightier than the breakers on the shore—the Lord above is mightier than these!" (Psalm 93:4 NLT)

He attends to minute detail—"You made all the delicate, inner parts of my body and knit me together in my mother's womb. Thank you for making me so wonderfully complex! Your workmanship is marvelous—how well I know it. You watched me as I was being formed in utter seclusion, as I was woven together in the dark of the womb. You saw me before I was born." (Psalm 139:13-16 NLT)

He is praised for His goodness—"Let each generation tell its children of your mighty acts; let them proclaim your power. I will meditate on your majestic, glorious splendor and your wonderful miracles. Your awe-inspiring deeds will be on every tongue; I will proclaim your greatness. Everyone will share the story of your wonderful goodness; they will sing with joy about your righteousness." (Psalm 145:4-7 NLT)

Those who experience awe first hand naturally feel compelled to share their experiences with others. That Core expression of wonderment is the breathless voice of the heart filled to overflowing from an encounter with the Creator. That awe brings us to the person and work of Christ who proves how much we are loved. Jesus, Creator God, died for you and me that we could be reconciled and welcomed into a relationship with a holy God.

As others observe these Core traits in you, undaunted by relational pressure, they are observing your Core identity choosing to honor your Creator. Others can see your Core self being executive in your life choices, actions, and values. As you show these characteristics and values consistently over time, in any place, and around any person, you are living intentionally from your Core being. That consistency is evidence of "Core integrity." Core integrity reflects an individual who intentionally desires his or her life to be to the praise of the Creator. This is observable in anyone who has encountered

God's love. Intention is a conscious activity of the Core self using the mind to live with purpose.

How does spiritual intent compare to material intent in human choice? When one lives from Core identity, choices are made based on one's internal convictions. Knowing we are finite requires a conscious awareness that we are dependent on our Creator for our needs, wishes, wants, and desires. Core faith recognizes that the Creator's love for humanity leads to impartial provision.

> "For he gives his sunlight to both the evil and the good, and he sends rain on the just and the unjust alike." (Matthew 5:45 NLT)

However, Paul assured believers by his testimony of faith...

> "This same God who takes care of me will supply all your needs from his glorious riches, which have been given to us in Christ Jesus." (Philippians 4:19 NLT)

The child of God can rest assured that needs will be provided through Jesus Christ. We are reminded of that truth by the psalmist.

> "Take delight in the Lord, and he will give you your heart's desires." (Psalm 34:4 NLT)

Living intentionally from our Core being, we communicate with the Creator regarding our needs and desires and He hears us.

James, the practical apostle, taught basic Christian living in simple terms. He wrote of those who operate from their Relational self without acknowledging the Creator as relevant to outcomes.

> "Look here, you who say, 'Today or tomorrow we are going to a certain town and will stay there a year. We will do business there and make a profit. How do you know what your life will be like tomorrow? Your life is like the morning fog—it's here a little while, then it's gone. What you ought to say is, 'If the Lord wants us to, we will live and do this or that.' Otherwise

you are boasting about your own pretentious plans, and all such boasting is evil." (James 4:13-16 NLT)

The Relational self makes plans without consideration of the Creator's role in one's daily provision. The Relational self arrogantly sees itself in charge of making plans and expecting profitable outcomes without even considering his own mortality.

Core identity lives in the conscious awareness that God provides for us based on His intimate knowledge of each of us. Therefore, we can make plans and take action in full awareness that our choices are made from reliance upon Him. This passage shows the difference between living from one's Core rather than one's Relational self. The Relational self lives solely from the material perspective and acts without thought of the Creator's purposeful involvement with humanity.

The third list represents those actions and activities that you pursue in life either to express your Core self or do because it defines your Relational identity. Your Relational identity can undermine your Core identity if you seek to please, to conform to, or to control others. The degree that happens reflects how you allow yourself to be defined—from within your being or by what others expect. The younger, the more frequent, and the more intense the definition of your Relational self was reinforced by your family of origin, the less likely it was for your Core identity to be in charge. The Relational identity may hold childhood messages that haunt the mind internally into adulthood. "Lazy, worthless, bad seed, good-for-nothing, a failure," are a few of the possible messages by which the Relational identity was shaped and reinforced. Others may see your Relational identity externally expressed as painful shyness or as prickly brashness. That social behavior shows the Relational self of a person who does not feel safe to express his Core identity in the presence of others.

Before two years of age, the child expresses the needs of her Creator-endowed identity by actions and sounds. Sensorimotor development is evident in that any sense of discomfort like hunger or thirst will result in utterances of sounds and physical actions to attempt to express Core need. When a need presents, she expresses by sounds of crying or whimpering out of discomfort or of screaming and kicking out of frustration. The Creator gave her that ability to express when in need, counting on the adults in her life to take notice and to provide for her as Jehovah Creator God lovingly provides for all of humanity.

Development of language gives the child two abilities: the first are words to communicate needs to the parental figure who provides her needs; the second are words that express autonomy like "No" or "Mine." The "terrible twos" pass quickly if the parent respects the child's identity differentiation and assertion and does not take such personally or see it as a sign of rebellion. Rebellion requires a level of understanding not present in a preschool or even a preadolescent child. Potty training is a clear example that the child will not learn to regulate her bodily functions by parental command. She must learn that self-control when she is capable and ready. Coercion by parental authority prolongs the child's inability to recognize her own body signals. Even if the parent knows her need to use the toilet, the child must learn from her Core being to listen to and regulate her own body.

In spiritual development, Core identity goes through a growth process under the direction of the Holy Spirit. Paul describes the process in his letter to a group of Galatian Christians who were feeling pressured from their Relational identity to conform to what others imposed on them. They were told that they were still subject to the Mosaic Law and circumcision to be in right standing with God. Paul shows them that the Holy Spirit was awakening them to living from their Core being and the evidence was shown by the presence of nine actions expressed intentionally.

> "But the Holy Spirit produces this kind of fruit in our lives: love, joy, peace, patience, kindness, goodness, faithfulness, gentleness, and self-control. (Galatians 5:22-23 NLT)

The fruits are not emotions, but rather actions taken which show Core intention displaying love, joy, peace, patience, kindness, goodness, faithfulness, gentleness, and self-control. Notice that the last phase of spiritual development is that of self-control. Paul is making this point: the work of the Holy Spirit within one's Core being results in growth not from coercion and fear, but Core self listening to the Holy Spirit. It is the result of growth from a loving relationship with God the Father by the atoning work of the Son through the manifest grace in the work of His Spirit. Core faith brings righteous obedience without fear. The mature believer, who operates from his Core being, manifests self-control in mind, body, and spirit.

The Organ of Core Expression—The Amazing Brain

We have explored identity from an integrative look at Biblical and scientific information regarding identity. Now I want to introduce you to an exciting concept based on the latest scientific findings. In this past decade, we have come to understand how our Core identity uses the brain to express itself. The human brain was designed by the Creator to serve our Core identity. Through it, we sustain life, learn about our world, understand self and others, remember what we need to know for life, and express our thoughts and feelings with the highest expression directed to our Creator. Understanding the design of the brain will help you to understand the organ that allows your Core identity to continue to exist, to make sense of experience, and to express who you truly are as intended by the Creator.

Advances in technology over the past decade allow scientists to observe, explore, and understand the human brain as never before. The beauty of the Creator's design is profoundly simply. Please don't be intimidated by this information. Follow along with me and become amazed by what you learn. The brain is designed to process information, provide reflexive reactions for survival, and provide intentional responses for expression. To accomplish this, three major areas of the brain are involved in processing information from the external world: the brain stem, the limbic system, and the cortex.

The brain stem is where the brain is connected to the body. The body has many special types of sensory cells that collect information from the person's environment. You may have learned the five senses that Aristotle identified around 350 BC—tasting, touching, smelling, seeing, and hearing. In reality, there are many more. Taste consists of five different senses: salt, sweet, bitter, sour, and savory. Touch includes four: pressure, temperature, pain, and itch. Some pose that the number of different senses may be from twenty to forty. The brain stem also serves the body by sending information to muscle groups with how to respond to the sensory information.

The nerves carry the sensory information to the brain stem where it enters and is passed along to the second area of the brain, the limbic system. A number of limbic structures function together to act as a communication center directing sense information to different areas for processing, to identify and respond if there is danger, to code memory for retention, to express emotion, to provide reward, to regulate body function, and to inform the cortex so options for action are identified.

The cortex is the thinking brain that processes sensory messages and provides options for physical response. It holds working memory for executive functions like how to plan, organize, prioritize, manage time, and orient the body in space. Association areas in the cortex assist with learning, memory, language, perception, and higher order functions. The cortex is involved in producing thoughts and holding beliefs on a conscious level.

As the following image shows, there are two directions that the brain processes information. Bottom-up or top-down processing both serve a purpose. Neither is good or bad; it is how the brain seeks to make sense of things in our environment.

Information Processing

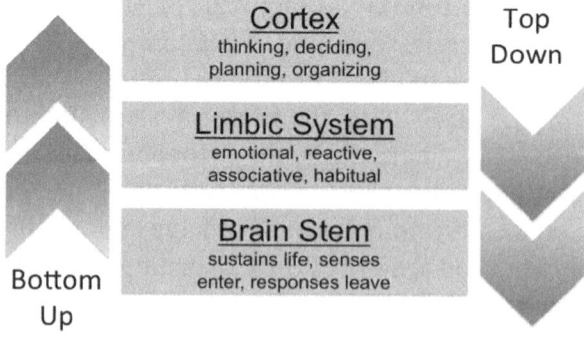

Bottom-up processing begins with information from the sensory network of the body entering the brain stem. When this information goes to the limbic system, it is passed to various areas throughout the brain. The fastest processors in the limbic brain are the amygdalae. If sensory information is associated to the emotion of fear, the amygdalae activate an alarm signal that broadcasts throughout the brain and body preparing for a defensive action against perceived danger.

Let's assume that a person was afraid of dogs as a child. While walking along a sidewalk in a residential area as an adult, the person sees a dog charging toward him. His amygdalae tell his body to stand still (the freeze response). In that moment, images of attacking dogs go through his mind. His paralysis becomes stronger. This bottom-up processing knows that he cannot run fast enough to escape the dog nor will getting angry at the dog protect him. His sympathetic nervous system responds to the alarm by increasing heart rate, blood pressure, adrenalin, and breathing to get energy to the muscles. He braces for those growling vicious jaws to clamp onto his legs or arms followed by pain.

Top-down processing kicks in moments after the alarm system is already activated. The thinking brain is not consulted by the amygdalae. The sensory information finally reaches the cortex where the thinking brain takes over. The cortex realizes that there is more to the image of the charging dog. The image broadens to include a leash attached to the dog's collar with an owner holding the leash to restrain the dog. The cortex collects more information from the senses. A whimpering sound of a small dog is heard behind him. The voice of a woman is heard reassuring her pet. The man turns to see the woman pick up a small dog and hold it in her arms. Based on additional sensory information collected from the environment, the cortex tells the amygdalae and other aspects of the limbic system that he is not the target and not in as much danger as assumed. The result is that the cortex speaks with the voice of reason and the limbic system quiets. Rational thought is now in charge, the parasympathetic nervous system can begin to quiet body and mind. Activated emotions can quiet and reflexive physical responses can rest.

The Relational self tends to use bottom-up processing, focusing on the environment. Emotions assigned to the sensory information from past negative experiences activate the amygdalae, bringing forward automatic responses from emotional memory to such circumstances. The Relational self is reflexive and reactive. The external world is its focus. Perceived rejection by others brings up fear responses that keep the Relational self trapped. Our Core identity is a top-down processor. Core beliefs, Core faith, the natural Core search for rational truth brings calming in the face of distress.

A Core relationship that focuses on the Creator and trusts in Him has a top-down benefit of emotional quieting and strengthening of Core identity. Isaiah wrote of this promise to any who place their trust is God.

"You will keep in perfect peace all who trust in you, all whose thoughts are fixed on you!" (Isaiah 26:3 NLT)

Paul writes of the believer who confronts the distressing emotions of anxiety and worry with prayer and faith and what the promised outcome will be.

"Don't worry about anything; instead, pray about everything. Tell God what you need, and thank him for all he has done. Then you will experience God's peace, which exceeds anything we can understand. His peace will guard your hearts and minds as you live in Christ Jesus." (Philippians 4:7 NLT)

These two verses are a starting point for you to search God's word for other top-down truth written to your Core self that will meet your needs bringing confidence, comfort, and peace. Isn't this amazing? The Creator had human beings write truth under the inspiration of the Spirit. These truths quiet the soul and spirit of those who live from their Core being. Our Core identity benefits from top-down processing, an innate part of the Creator's design of the human brain. Doesn't that bring you to awe? These principles can intervene in addictions and negative habits, the symptoms of living from one's Relational self.

Bottom-up processing activates another structure in the limbic system, the hippocampus. With bottom-up processing, rewards may be falsely assigned to habits that are emotionally charged. Those wrongly associated rewards lead people to pursue substances or behavior that will only temporarily soothe the Relational self. The Relational self cannot delay gratification; it must have the "feel-good" state right now. From top-down processing, Our Core self uses the higher brain functions of the cortex to be intentional and to seek accountability relationships that will support the Core self as it breaks the imprisoning habits.

We find that Jesus used the different processing pathways of the brain to reach His audience. He told stories that were often heard by the Relational self of the listener. Ideas that are new rely on bottom-up processing. Jesus' stories were rich with sensory information. On one occasion, the crowd was hungry and hungry people don't listen too well. Jesus fed the multitudes to allow reason to aid in understanding. When the bottom-up processor is no longer hungry, the cortex can begin to think about the stories Jesus told and assign meaning to the ones that spoke to them. When the disciples approached Jesus with questions about the stories He told, He would explain the meanings of the stories so the disciples could process the stories from top-down.

The Pharisees would ask Jesus questions that showed their bottom-up perceptions. One bottom-up process question the Pharisees asked, "Should we pay taxes to Rome?" The Pharisees did not like paying tribute to Rome. However, to avoid paying meant a severe consequence. The Pharisees asked this question to trap Jesus. In their bottom-up processing, they could not conceive a rational response. If Jesus answered "No," they could have turned him over to Roman soldiers for public insurrection. If Jesus said, "Yes," they could have turned Him over to the Sanhedrin for teaching heresy.

Jesus gives the Pharisees the top-down answer, "Whose face is that on this coin? Give back to Caesar that which is Caesar's. But give to God what is God's." Hate and fear were evoked in them regarding the subject of taxes and the consequence of not paying. In each confrontation with the Pharisees, Jesus as the incarnate Creator was using His physical brain as He had designed it. By the means of top-down processing He knew they wished to trap him. He answered from the standpoint of logic and reason, which left them dumbfounded.

The integration of both means of processing, bottom-up and top-down, is possible to a person of faith. Paul illustrates this impossible concept only doable if one is living from Core faith. He says "...true godliness with contentment is itself great wealth." (1 Timothy 6:6 NLT) Paul is posing a paradox that no human being can attain in their Relational self—to be both godly and content. Godliness, or God-likeness, requires a human being to be holy, which means perfect, as the Creator. Our Relational self is vigilant waiting for a mistake to be made and worst of all, for it to be pointed out.

The more one pays attention to possible failure, the more likely a mistake will be made. When a mistake is made, the natural result will be unhappiness with one's self. Faith in Christ is the means of resolving this seeming impossibility. We know, in our Core being because of the death of Jesus, we are cleansed and forgiven. Our rational mind knows that to be cleansed and forgiven in the depths of our being, we are reconciled to God the Father. We also know that if we sin and come to Christ in confession, the atoning work of God the Son continues to keep us holy before God the Father. God the Spirit seals our relationship and leads our learning and development to maturity in Christ. The result of God the Spirit living within us is observable change called the fruits of a Spirit-filled life.

> "But the Holy Spirit produces this kind of fruit in our lives: love, joy, peace, patience, kindness, goodness, faithfulness, gentleness, and self-control. There is no law against these things!" (Galatians 5:22-23 NLT)

The presence of these fruits manifested by our Core being displays contentment to all who know us. Godliness and contentment coexist in our Core being because the Spirit of the Creator indwells us. The outcome is a life with incredible richness, all through the person of Jesus Christ.

36

A Practical Exercise to Bring Mind and Body Together

God-likeness is the Core desire of the believer who seeks to honor the Creator in all choices and actions. Core faith knows cognitively what the right actions are. However a problem arises. The Apostle Paul expressed his frustration over this in Romans 7. The recurring sin habits of his Relational self or his old nature overruled his Core desire. The limbic thinking of the Relational self had to be quieted by top-down processing from the truth of Romans 8.

"So now there is no condemnation for those who belong to Christ Jesus. And because you belong to him, the power of the life-giving Spirit has freed you from the power of sin that leads to death." (Romans 8:1-2 NLT)

Only then could the believer experience in his or her Core being the limbic calming of God's peace.

The following is an example of how to experience such calming through mindful breathing. This is how to retrain your limbic system to return to calmness after stress. The Relational self or the old nature developed sin habits through life experiences of judgment. These judgments and criticisms reinforced feelings of fear, doubt, anger, and shame. This is the result of the bottom-up processing our brains do to protect us from perceived danger. The reaction of the amygdalae to sensed threat is freeze, flee, or fight. If the pattern of danger happens frequently, the hippocampus stores the emotional memory and identifies danger by associations that are parallel in nature. Our limbic system develops habits of reacting without the logic of top-down processing and lacks insight and truth. Those habits lose their power when replaced with limbic calming, freeing the brain to return to top-down processing.

The following exercise is designed to assist in limbic calming. It may be more helpful if you record the following script and listen to the recording of your own voice to guide you through the exercise. These instructions are intended as an example of how to use limbic calming and experience the benefits.

Mindful Breathing Script Begins

As you begin, allow yourself to breathe slowly and deep. Welcome each breath as you take it in for a count of four, hold it for a count of four, and now release that breath for a count of four. Continue this pattern of mindful breathing. Take in each breath, hold it briefly, and release it fully.

Continue to breathe slowly in that manner. As you continue, you may notice how different each breath can be. Each breath provides refreshment throughout the body. Every cell of your brain and body is nurtured. You are aware that breathing is a natural process. The brain stem keeps you breathing without conscious effort to keep you alive. That is an amazing aspect of the Creator's design.

As you consciously breathe, thoughts or feelings may enter your awareness and distract your attention. Just let go of these distractions. Bring your awareness back to your pattern of relaxed breathing. Those thoughts and feelings that interrupt are habits that are not needed during this time of quiet meditation, relaxed breathing, and growing calmness.

As you consciously become aware of each breath, you notice a sense of calmness take place. The limbic system, the emotional brain, can take time to rest. Allow yourself some time to experience and enjoy the calmness that conscious breathing brings. Your Core being notices that in this mindful moment of conscious breath, in this moments of stillness, you can be executive in your mind and body because of how the Creator designed you.

In that stillness of mind, you encounter the Creator's design. He formed you in His image and breathed into you life and spirit. The Creator sees your struggles and gently says, "Cease striving and know that I am God..." (Psalm 46:10 NASB) Based on that promise, scripture says, "You will experience God's peace, which exceeds anything we can understand. His peace will guard your hearts and minds as you live in Christ Jesus." (Philippians 4:7 NLT)

Each breath you take you can direct to different places in your body. Focus on one area at a time. Allow your breath to wash over the area. Allow that area to relax to the degree that is comfortable. Do not force the body to relax and be calm. Just allow it to happen. It will come as it is ready. Breathing will bring calmness to the area where you direct it.

Just this much may be enough for now. As you continue, mindful of the calmness, assert these truths—I am safe; I am accepted; I am forgiven; I am. Then as you are ready, bring however much calmness you desire with you as your focus turns outward once again.

Mindful Breathing Script Ends

Using Paul's words from Philippians 4:9 NLT, "Keep putting into practice all you learned and received from me...Then the God of peace will be with you." As you practice the things I have shared with you in this book you will eperience the peace of God. The mindful breathing will also be a powerful tool in reducing your stress, releasing your habits, and restoring your body and brain to enjoy comfort and peace.

This Frees Us for Core Expression

As you read on, we will look into two forms of expression that were part of the Creator's original design and the ultimate response that the Creator desired from His creation. I remind you again that the Creator did not need this response from creation; this was His desire and His right. Paul stated this quite clearly in his defense when he was brought before the Council in Athens.

> "Since he is Lord of heaven and earth, he doesn't live in man-made temples, and human hands can't serve his needs—for he has no needs. He himself gives life and breath to every-thing, and he satisfies every need." (Acts 17:24-25 NLT)

The Creator, on completion of creation, set aside a day of rest. The day was blessed and sanctified. All creation was to bless the Creator, which meant "to bow the knee" in reverence to Him. All creation was to praise Him for His mighty works.

As we proceed, we will explore how our Core identity was hard-wired to express praise to our Creator through service and worship. The outcome of expressing service and worship has wonderful benefits in producing spiritual maturity, recognizing God's direction, experiencing abundant joy, and encountering indescribable awe. This is the ultimate demonstration of our Core self using top-down and bottom-up processing in an integrated manner in service and worship that glorifies our Creator.

Section 3.2: The Core Expression of Service

[What personal traits identify an ideal servant? How would the ideal servant relate to those he serves? Why would someone desire to serve? In all of humanity, where might the ideal servant be found?

Servants might be captured and forced to serve with meager room and board their only reward. Some may serve in positions of leadership for altruistic reasons that benefit humanity. Still others serve for the wealth and power that they will gain.

Think of what it might be like to serve as an expression of gratitude. Through serving you may find an avenue to express who you are and communicate what is truly important. Fully aware that service is not always a pleasant task, you serve in anticipation of the outcome—joy.

God enjoys humanity and sometime laughs at the antics we use to justify our beliefs. God uses irony to communicate a simple message. As stated in Chapter Three of Book One, the message that humanity is to learn from the Cross of Christ is ridiculous to humanity. It defies logic or power. It befuddles wisdom; it deflates strength. Service as an expression from one's Core being is such a divine irony. May it lead us to Awe!]

Chapter 2:

PAUL – THE MAKING OF A SERVANT

Keep your journal close as you read this narrative on the Apostle Paul. Be mindful of the thoughts and feelings from your Core self prompted by the Holy Spirit. Record these thoughts in your journal for future contemplation.

The Merchant's Son from Tarsus

The year was about 5 A.D. (Anno Domini) by Christian reckoning. The birth of a son to a Jewish family of the diaspora in the city of Tarsus, in the country of Cilicia, in Asia Minor, was a joyous occasion. Saul Paulus was so named to reflect his dual citizenship as both Jew and Roman. His family was of the tribe of Benjamin like his namesake, King Saul. The land of Israel was quite a distance from Tarsus where the family currently lived. Thoughts of the homeland of Israel brought grief and longing. The tenth day of the tenth month of the Jewish calendar was a day of fasting in remembrance of the Babylonian siege on Jerusalem and the destruction of Solomon's Temple.

Jehovah God had allowed Nebuchadnezzar to conquer Israel because they had turned to worship pagan gods. The people were taken as slaves to Babylon far from the Land of Promise, from the City of Jerusalem, and from the Temple of Solomon where God dwelt among them. In time, another conqueror subdued Babylon. The new conqueror allowed some of the tribes to return to Israel while others were moved to other places in Syria as slaves. That was how Saul's family came to Cilicia in Asia Minor.

Two more world empires conquered Asia Minor where Saul's ancestors lived. The Greeks were first, bringing the Greek language and culture to the region. The Greeks believed that anyone who did not speak Greek was less intelligent, lacking reason, and driven by emotions. So, the Greeks conquered the "barbarians" and civilized them with Grecian language, arts, sciences, and philosophies. The Grecian Empire absorbed the technical knowledge they discovered among the barbarians. The conquered areas stretched as far east as India, which included the Medo-Persian Empire of Asia and then South to Israel, Arabia, and Egypt. The common language shared by the citizens of Tarsus in Saul's day was Koine Greek.

When the Roman Empire conquered the Grecian dynasty, the Romans contributed their legal and political culture. The world learned that all citizens of the Roman Empire had rights that could not be taken from them no matter where they lived in the Empire. Caesar granted citizenship to leading families of Cilicia sixty years prior to Saul's birth. His grandfather had socioeconomic status in Tarsus that made him eligible for Roman citizenship. His son and grandson were naturalized citizens of the Roman Empire by birth. Why is that important? Wait until later in the story. It will become one of God's ironies.

Cilicia was part of Asia Minor, which shows how widespread was the Greco-Roman culture of Mediterranean Europe. When the Romans conquered the Grecian Empire, they did not attempt to change the Grecian culture that stood for centuries in distant lands. The Romans demonstrated their skill in the political sciences. By granting citizenship to those of social status in conquered countries, an allegiance to Rome could be counted on. The political wisdom of the Romans incorporated the Grecian and national cultures of the conquered rather than replace them. The Roman Empire's ability to organize regional governments, establish courts of justice, and enforce Roman law gave them political control over a vast land area. The Roman Empire was almost twice the land holdings of the Greeks.

That included Europe, the British Isles, Asia Minor, Palestine, Egypt, and North African countries. The Roman Empire included all the countries bordering the Mediterranean Sea.

Saul grew up with an awareness of the similarities and differences of Jewish and Gentile cultures. Human nature was the same in both cultures. Those with power made and interpreted the laws. Both Roman and Hebrew leaders in Cilicia would declare they were the servants of the people by means of the Law. These leaders asserted how they believed Roman or Hebrew Law should be applied. Few leaders in either culture were truly humble. Leaders in Greek, Roman, and Hebrew cultures believed that those of position or status served as authority over the people to maintain social order and peace. They believed their status and its related responsibilities entitled them to be served in return.

Saul's education began at home. As directed by Moses, Saul grew up with the detailed teachings of the Torah, of the Law of Moses, and of Jehovah, the God of Israel who delivered Israel from slavery in Egypt. Saul's parents knew the summary passages of God's Law and were guided by it.

> "Listen, O Israel! The Lord is our God, the Lord alone. And you must love the Lord your God with all your heart, all your soul, and all your strength. And you must commit yourselves wholeheartedly to these commands that I am giving you today. Repeat them again and again to your children. Talk about them when you are at home and when you are on the road, when you are going to bed and when you are getting up. Tie them to your hands and wear them on your forehead as reminders. Write them on the doorposts of your house and on your gates." (Deuteronomy 6:4-9 NLT)

Saul grew up witnessing his father's commitment to the Torah by his faithful application of these verses. The family spoke Hebrew at home and read from Torah at home and at the synagogue, their place of worship. Father was a Pharisee who wore the unique attire of his status. At times of prayer and worship, Saul's father would take a tallit, a prayer shawl, carefully drape it over his shoulders, and with a well-practiced gesture bring it over his head. As he donned the tallit, Father would pray, "Blessed are you, Lord, our God, sovereign of the universe Who has sanctified us with His commandments and commanded us to wrap ourselves in the tallit."[4] Father would then don the tefillin which was a thin strap that was wound on the non-dominant arm and hand and say, "Blessed are you, Lord, our God, sovereign of the universe Who has sanctified us with His commandments and commanded us to put on tefillin."[4] Next, he would place the phylactery, a small box containing a paper with a verse on it, on his forehead held by straps around his head while reciting, "Blessed are you, Lord, our God, sovereign of the universe Who has sanctified us with His commandments and commanded about the mitzvah of tefillin. Blessed be the Name of His glorious kingdom forever and ever."[4] Each morning and on the Sabbath, Saul's father expressed his devotion to Jehovah in this way. When the family expression of worship to Jehovah was complete, these objects were removed with ceremony and carefully put away.

On occasion, Father would continue to wear the phylactery for weeks at a time. "Father?" Saul once asked. "Why do you wear that box on your forehead?" Deuteronomy 6 spoke about this as one of those teaching moments in which parents are to share about God and His Law. Saul's father explained to his son that the phylactery on his forehead kept him mindful of Jehovah and His Law. As he felt it tap his forehead through the day, Jehovah came to mind. He stopped and reflected for a moment on whether his actions were honoring to Jehovah. Saul was not embarrassed by his father's attire because other Pharisees wore the robes and phylacteries in public. Their clothing identified their social status, just like the red and gold robes of Roman patricians or the white togas of the Greek scholars.

Because of the small size of the Jewish community in the towns of the diaspora, the religious leaders could not rely on their community to pay them to provide education as was done in Israel. To provide for their families they took up vocations of manual crafts. Some of the Pharisees of Tarsus known by their garb were respected merchants in the Tarsian community. Saul's grandfather and father had the skill of weaving the cloth used in tent-making to earn a living. They also had the intellectual ability to teach the Torah in precise detail.

Saul's grandfather and father became wealthy merchants from marketing their unique product—cilicium. A unique breed of long-haired goats lived a few miles outside of the city in the Tarsus Mountains. These goats were not like the domestic breed of goats near the village of Angora. Angora goats had long soft white hair that was shorn twice each year, processed into thread, and woven into the desired fabric—Mohair. This durable fabric had a silk-like sheen with a natural beauty. Clothing of mohair insulated the wearer from the winter cold and the summer heat. It felt good next to the skin.

The Cilician goats, also shorn twice each year, had long black hair that was coarse and tough. The durable fabric woven from that goat hair was called cilicium. It was highly valued for the making of sails, sackcloth, and tents. This coarse material stood up to the elements of wind, rain, and extremes of temperature lasting for years. As a dwelling, it provided warmth in the winter cold and coolness from the summer heat. Cilicium was the cloth used by the Paulus family in their tent-making industry.

Because Tarsus was located near the Cilician Gates, a pass in the Tarsus Mountains to the north and the Tarsus harbor to the south, the Paulus family had the ideal location to export their goods. The Cilician Gates were used by the Roman military as a transport route to Italy, Greece, Syria, Palestine, Egypt, and the north coast of Africa. On occasion, a Centurion sought out the Paulus family shop in the Agora to place an order for military tents. A Phoenician ship captain might be seen haggling over the price of sailcloth. A bashi was arranging for his camel caravan to take tents to the nomadic tribes of Asia Minor, the Arabian Peninsula, and North Africa. The nomads used tents for their dwellings, valuing their durability and ease of transport.

An old Jewish proverb was the rationale for teaching one's son a trade—"He who does not teach his son a trade, teaches him to be a thief."[5] When Saul was old enough, his father took him as an apprentice to learn the craft of tent making. Saul worked in the family shop learning the different skills required to make the fabric, to cut out the panels, and to sew them together to make sails or tents. After a day of handling the large panels of cilicium, Saul was itching all over.

At first, his hands would become cracked and bleed from handling the coarse fabric. But his hands toughened with the passing of time, adapting to what the job required.

After the Roman conquest of Cilicia, Tarsus placed increasing value on academics. The schools and universities of Tarsus gained status greater than Athens and Alexandria during the time of Saul. This was yet another part of the Creator's plan, another feature of God's irony. The value placed on education in the Tarsian community meant children of the merchants, nobles, and any other citizens, who could find the means, were given a broad liberal education. Saul's family wanted him to build on his foundational understanding of Torah as preparation to take over the family business. This would equip Saul with the skills to market their cilicium products to the Gentile cultures around. So Saul was provided a tutor, a learned slave from a conquered country, knowledgeable in the Grecian culture.

Saul's education as an adolescent was multi-faceted. The day began at home with morning prayer and breakfast with his family. Saul met his tutor at a stoa to discuss his assignment on the classics, science, or philosophy. He went to his apprenticeship to work and learn the family trade. From time to time, Saul enjoyed athletic activities at the gymnasium. Saul's adolescent life was a rich, active one; he did not express any dissent or complaint.

The rationale for Saul's father and grandfather providing these opportunities for Saul was based on Jehovah's covenant promise to Father Abraham. They wanted Saul to be equipped to live by that covenant promise in his dealings with the Gentiles.

> "I will make you into a great nation. I will bless you and make you famous, and you will be a blessing to others. I will bless those who bless you and curse those who treat you with contempt. All the families on earth will be blessed through you." (Genesis 12:1-3 NLT)

The experience of exile from Israel, Jerusalem, and the Temple resulted in a greater faithfulness from the children of Israel to Jehovah and His Law. They were no longer turning to idols as they had. Jews of the diaspora were known by nations in which they lived to be different in their worship of Jehovah. Those countries that accepted Jehovah's people found themselves blessed in return. Cilicia was one such country.

Two hundred fifty years before Saul's birth, the Babylonian Talmud tells an amazing story of the Greek translation of Tanakh. King Ptolemy (Grecian King of Egypt) once gathered 72 Elders. He placed them in 72 different chambers without revealing to them why they were summoned. He entered each one's room and said: "Write for me the Torah of Moshe, your teacher." God put it in the heart of each one to translate identically as all the others did. The Spirit of God preserved His Word as the elders translated it.[6]

The Roman influence came about one hundred fifty years before Saul with the title becoming the Latin word meaning Seventy, Septuagint or by the numerical symbol, LXX. Because of the Roman spread of the Greek translation from the Library of Alexandria, Saul and his peers had the privilege at synagogue school to read and write Greek while learning from the Greek translation of the Tanakh.

Saul, in his adolescence, was provided a slave as a tutor to educate him in the knowledge of the secular world. This knowledge was seen as important for understanding the family business practices and the global market. It provided Saul with the ability to learn critical thinking. His father's shop was in the Agora, the Greek word for marketplace. Saul had a window on the world as people passed by. His tutor would take him to learn first hand what he was hearing from the shop. New activities took place each day. On one occasion, Saul heard students from the university at a stoa, a porch of a public building, debating different philosophical ideas. On another day, poetry and other literary classics were read. The gymnasium down the street was where sports events were conducted and athletes practiced for upcoming contests. Under the tutelage of his pedagogue, Saul learned how to communicate ideas to others in a persuasive way. All these experiences became useful resources throughout Saul's life. Saul grew up in a rich environment that gave him insight into many cultural ideas and practices. Through it all, Saul placed the greatest personal value on his education from the Tanakh, which included three types of literature—Teachings (Torah in Hebrew or Pentateuch in Greek), Prophets, and Writings.

✍ *Journal Time—How Does the History of Paul Increase Your Awe?*

Resolved to Serve God's Law

I was twenty-nine years of age when I boarded ship in the harbor of Tarsus. The ladings of cilicium, grains, wines, and brass were loaded into the hold the day before departure. I said goodbyes to the family in the night because I had to be on board at the break of dawn as the tide went out. I loved learning and was going to Jerusalem to attend the school of Gamaliel to become a lawyer. I was going to learn from one of the great men of the Sanhedrin, the Jewish Elders who led in areas of law, doctrine, and matters of justice.

As dawn broke, the ship was loosed from its moorings. The strength of the morning tide drew the ship away from the dock as it retreated out to the open sea. As the sails were hoisted, I stood at the rail watching the harbor shrink into the distance. The ship followed the coast, stopping for a day and night at Seleucia to exchange passengers and goods. Arrival at Caesarea was a breathtaking sight. The two hundred and eighty mile journey only took seven days. King Herod of Israel had rebuilt the port as a deep sea harbor with storerooms, temples, baths, and imposing public buildings.

I had a mix of feelings but the strongest was eagerness to meet with Gamaliel the Elder who would tutor me to complete my doctorate in Torah Law. Gamaliel was a tolerant man with amazing insight and wisdom; he could see the wisest course of action in problems. He would speak with confident wisdom from God in a quiet manner and with a humble spirit. My goal was to become a member of the Great Sanhedrin, the High Council at the Temple in Jerusalem. My convictions were with the Pharisee party.

Most of us Pharisees considered ourselves unquestionable authorities on the Tanakh and the Oral Traditions of Israel. We served the Law of God. We were quick to show a law-breaker the infraction and let the sinner know that obedience to our ruling would solve the personal ongoing sin problem. We used our status to prove our rightful position as servant to God's Law. In my perception, my life and future was in place; I had wisdom from which to adjudicate; I was an exemplary Hebrew of Hebrews. I enjoyed life in Jerusalem; but I did long for the Greco-Roman culture of Tarsus. The presence of the Roman soldiers against the stark Jewish culture of Jerusalem was rather oppressive. In Tarsus the presence of Roman soldiers were only those en route. Cilicia as a country was granted independence by Rome and was sovereign in its own affairs.

King Herod, a Jewish king reigning with permission from Rome, built the majestic seaport of Caesarea. Herod rebuilt the second Temple that replaced the one destroyed by Nebuchadnezzar. Herod's Temple stood out with a beauty that outshined other constructions of Herod. Herod wanted Jerusalem to reflect his majesty. Because the condition of the second temple was poor, Herod rebuilt it into an edifice that would make him proud. I worshipped at Herod's Temple on the ceremonial days. Herod's Temple reflected the magnificence of Grecian architecture familiar from home.

My friends and I from Asia Minor attended the Synagogue of the Freed Slaves in Jerusalem. Hellenized Jews, raised in the Greek culture of Cilicia, came together in this synagogue to read and speak about the Torah in our native tongue. Natives of Jerusalem primarily spoke Hebrew, so it was a comfort to speak Greek with others knowledgeable in the Torah. We had the gusto of the Grecian style of philosophical debate when arguing the meanings of passages from Torah. On one particular day, a man from Cilicia named Stephen stood in response to the Torah reading of the day. Stephen began to use the scripture reading to prove that a man named Jesus was Messiah.

Stephen emphasized that this man called Jesus from the town of Nazareth, a small community in Galilee, was the Anointed One of God for whom Israel waited. I who was a learned man accepting of many cultures knew the prejudice toward one from Nazareth. The people of the Nazareth area were so crude in manner and speech that even their fellow Galileans looked down on them. This Jesus had been a Nazarene and had been crucified for blasphemy just a couple years before I came to Jerusalem. For Stephen to assert that this man from Nazareth could be Messiah was laughable. Stephen stated he was a follower of this Jesus and invited others to join him as a follower as well. This "Nazarene" cult was a concern that we Pharisees discussed in the high council of the Sanhedrin.

Gamaliel the Elder, the dean of the school I attended, was also the head of the Great Sanhedrin. Gamaliel advocated on behalf of the leaders of this Nazarene cult that was growing in Jerusalem. These men and women were adamant that this man Jesus was the Messiah and that after His crucifixion and burial, He was raised from the dead. This Jesus was crucified for His blasphemy because of His claims that He was God. He would have been stoned to death if it had been the decision of the Temple Council. The Pharisees were hoping to have the Romans handle the matter as an insurrection against Roman authority to keep the Jewish leaders out of it as much as possible.

Gamaliel spoke with the voice of reason and tolerance as the Sanhedrin became increasingly concerned. Other members of the Sanhedrin were convinced that action had to be taken toward the leaders of this cult. These leaders would speak in the Temple and the synagogues about this Jesus quoting the Torah, the Prophets, and the Writings in defense of their beliefs. Gamaliel gave historical examples as evidence that movements of this sort were short lived. Theudas who lived eighty years before claimed to be God's anointed. After his death, Theudas' followers drifted off and that group became extinct. Gamaliel also reminded us of Judas of Galilee who proclaimed himself as God's anointed thirty years ago. When Judas of Galilee died, his followers dwindled away. Gamaliel spoke to what he believed was the wisest course of action regarding the Nazarene cult.

> "My advice is, leave these men alone. Let them go. If they are planning and doing these things merely on their own, it will soon be overthrown. But if it is from God, you will not be able to overthrow them. You may even find yourselves fighting against God!" (Acts 5:9, 10 NLT)

Gamaliel's advice was not what we wanted to hear. The cult members who were Hellenized Jews were difficult to debate with and win. Even I found debate with the leaders of the Nazarenes frustrating. Stephen rankled my friends and me because of that. In retrospect, my pride was one of the reasons for my growing anger. Thus with Greek logic, if you cannot win, kill your opponent. We set in motion a plan to find people willing to perjure themselves to bring charges against Stephen. When the perjurers presented the charges to the members of the Sanhedrin, Stephen was arrested and brought before the High Council.

✍ *Journal Time—Why Was the Wisdom of Gamaliel Ignored?*

As the accusations against Stephen were voiced, all of us in the Council Chamber saw Stephen's whole countenance change. His face glowed like an angel's. He began to speak of the great historical figures of Israel and their faith. He spoke about Israel's repeated rebellion against Jehovah and murdering His prophets that warned Israel to turn from idols and back to Jehovah. Then he called us murders of the Messiah. This was the tipping point resulting in an outburst of rage from all in the Council chambers.

Stephen looked up toward the chamber ceiling and claimed to see this man Jesus standing in the presence of God. All of us as the leaders of the Sanhedrin covered our ears. The next moments were surreal. Some council members grabbed Stephen by the coat and dragged him from the court into the streets and out of the city. The rest of us followed in the knowledge that justice by the law was imminent. We would witness this blasphemer justly punished by stoning for his heinous sin of blasphemy. My mentors and friends were enraged as I was at the strong words of Stephen saying that we were "Messiah-killers."

One by one, my peers dropped their cloaks at my feet for me to tend while they administered the required punishment of death by stoning for Stephen's crime of blasphemy against God. With stones striking his body, his face misshapen, blood saturating his clothing, his extremities broken and dangling, Stephen once again looked upward and prayed, "Lord Jesus, receive my spirit." He fell to his knees, shouting, "Lord, don't charge them with this sin!" And with that, he died.

No, his last words did not quiet my rage. In that moment, I made a resolve to serve God's Law to end this blasphemy. I determined that I would personally wipe the name of Jesus and any who followed Him from the face of the Earth. Gamaliel may have encouraged tolerance with the Nazarene movement, believing in a natural death to the movement; but not I. I was faithful to the Law of Moses. I believed in Messiah; but this Jesus could not be He.

I enlisted men of the Sanhedrin to join me in removing the Nazarenes from Herod's Temple and to stop them from speaking of Jesus in the synagogues of Jerusalem. If any refused to comply, we would forcibly remove them and put them in jail. I expanded our efforts to identify anyone in Jerusalem who believed that Jesus was the resurrected Messiah. I began a house-to-house search to find those of the Nazarene Cult. We knocked on the door of each house and asked if anyone in that house believed in Jesus as the Messiah. True followers of Jesus answered without shame or dread. They seemed to have no fear to be identified with Him. As we found cult members, we arrested them and turned them over to the Temple Guards for imprisonment until trial.

Each day my squad searched Jerusalem from house to house and found men and women who were followers of Jesus of Nazareth. Their numbers were surprising. The jails filled quickly at first. Members of the Nazarene Cult were given the death sentence of stoning for blasphemy. They were dragged from the courtroom and stoned to death outside the city like Stephen. As time went by, the numbers decreased. I believed we were making strides in stopping this cult movement. I proudly served God's Law as a servant of Godly justice. I was meting out that which honored the Law of Moses.

I was heartsick when I heard that the reason for the decrease in the number of Nazarenes was that they just left Jerusalem. They were spreading into the countries surrounding Israel to avoid death. I approached the High Priest with a request for letters of introduction and endorsement signed by him so we could roust out those who moved north to Damascus. With the letters, we could encourage faithful Jews in the synagogues of Damascus to assist in the identification and arrest of the Nazarenes there. I planned to put any followers of this Jesus in chains and bring them back to Jerusalem for trial. We were going to stop this blasphemous movement now!

Armed with the letters, my entourage began the one hundred thirty-five mile march to Damascus. Our zeal made the miles pass quickly. We spoke of the plans of action upon our arrival in Damascus. My passion was contagious among my followers. We wanted to have the element of surprise to catch as many off guard as possible.

Blinded to See the Truth

I could see Damascus in the distance and anticipated arrival by midday. A mix of emotions flowed over and through me; excitement for our mission, anxiety for our success, anger at the thought of this blasphemy. I was not thinking like a self-controlled Stoic whose logic and objectivity governed his passions. The Stoic philosophers in the Agora of Tarsus would say that the salvation of humanity came through moderation, objectivity, and wisdom. Come to think of it, Gamaliel sounded too much like a stoic to me with his accepting approach. I was a servant to the Law of Moses and justice was my means to preserve Israel for God. Moderation would send the wrong message, allowing people to compromise the importance of the Law. I served the Law with my actions that I intended to keep the Hebrew nation faithful to the Law of Moses.

Then, without warning, a light from heaven shined down on and closely around me. The effect of the light was paralyzing. I lost all muscle tone and I collapsed to the ground. In that moment, I met that amazing man, who changed my life and transformed my mind. I heard a distinct voice speak from heaven, "Saul! Saul! Why are you persecuting me?"

"Who are you, lord?" I asked.

To that the voice replied, "I am Jesus, the one you are persecuting! Now, get up and go into the city, and you will be told what you must do." This amazing person is the self same person whose name I sought to extinguish from the lips of the Nazarene cult members. Jesus the Messiah called to me identifying me by name. Then He gave me a directive, to enter the city and wait for instructions on what I must do. The words were definite. There was a course of action planned for me to carry out.

All of my entourage saw the light fall on me alone, saw me collapse to my knees, and then heard a voice speak without knowing what was said. I stood up ready to obey what Jesus told me to do, opened my eyes, and found myself totally blind. I, the leader with a vision that others followed, was now blind and had to be led. I was led into the city to the home of Judas on Straight Street. I had planned to begin my campaign against the Nazarene cult in Judas' home. Instead, I sat in Judas' house, totally blind, without appetite, just waiting as Jesus asked me to do. My letters from the High Priest could do me no good in my present condition. In my mind, I kept trying to make sense of what happened just outside of the city.

Three days had passed when there was a knock at the door. Judas went to the door to welcome the unknown guest. "Is a man named Saul from Jerusalem staying with you?"

"Yes, why do you ask," was my host's reply.

"I am Ananias, I have a message for Saul. I am to pray for the return of his sight." Led to my room, Ananias introduced himself. "Brother Saul, the Lord Jesus has sent me to you so you may regain your sight and be filled with the Holy Spirit."

Ananias prayed to Jehovah that my eyes would be made to see again. He prayed that by the name of Jesus, the risen Messiah, my sight would be restored. After three days of total blindness, something like scales fell off my eyes and I could see once more. I rose with joy because the very name I wished to eradicate became the signs to me a Jew and the wonders to me a Gentile that sealed the truth for me. Jesus of Nazareth was the risen Messiah. My appetite returned. I ate and my energy was restored.

I asked to be baptized there and then as a public confession of my conversion. When Gentiles wanted to become Jews, baptism was a public witness that they were rejecting the pagan gods of their heritage, turning to Jehovah, and willingly submitting to the Law of God. I was a Jew of Jews and I asked to be baptized in the name of Jesus Christ, identifying with Him in death. I was an expert on what the Mosaic Law required for Jehovah God to see me holy before Him. Meeting Jesus Christ taught me of Jehovah's loving kindness, His incredible patience, and His redeeming grace. Through Jesus' shed blood at the cross on Calvary, I was made holy in Jehovah's sight.

What happened next came natural to me. I went to one of the synagogues in Damascus where I carried letters of introduction that I had intended for a different purpose. I listened to the reading from the Torah from Isaiah that day. Isaiah was a favorite prophet of mine. I was astounded by the relevance to Jesus. The eyes and ears of my heart heard the words of the Torah containing such life and such meaning that I had never noticed before. The Holy Spirit had opened the ears and eyes of my heart. As each phrase was read, my mind and heart were stirred. I became even more alive in the awe of Jehovah's plan. I could really relate to what the Prophet Jeremiah meant when he said, "When I discovered your words, I devoured them. They are my joy and my heart's delight, for I bear your name, O Lord God of Heaven's Armies." (Jeremiah 15:16 NLT)

When opportunity came in the service, I stood as a member of the Sanhedrin to share an interpretation of the Torah reading. I spoke of Isaiah's prophecy of the Messiah that He first had to suffer as the Servant to bring atonement for humanity's sin; how He was beaten that by His bruises He made us whole; how He was whipped that by His stripes we may find healing.

✍ *Journal Time—How Did Accepting Jesus Christ Change You?*

Even as I spoke, the Holy Spirit opened the eyes of my heart and brought more passages to mind. In later reflection on my thoughts of that day and my boldness, I realized that the Holy Spirit was at work in me and was speaking through me. I was no longer a servant of the Law, no longer a servant of the Sanhedrin, no longer a servant to my religious zeal that wanted to quash the Name of Jesus. I was a bondservant of Jesus Christ, the suffering Messiah, the Son of God. I would serve God by telling everyone who would hear the Good News that through faith in Jesus Christ we are cleansed from sin.

From that moment, I began to preach Jesus Christ as the Anointed One, the resurrected Lord. Words that I wrote much later described my transformed state of mind, "I am not ashamed of the Gospel of Jesus Christ. It is the power of God by which I received salvation." (Romans 1:16 NLT) That is when I truly began to live from my Core Being as Jesus had intended all along. I met Jesus and in so doing was introduced to my Core being by Him. This was my true identity that He my Creator intended for me even before the world was created. Isaiah said "The Lord called me before my birth; from within the womb he called me by name.." (Isaiah 49:1 NLT)

I now recognized that the same Jesus that I had been persecuting was Messiah and He was alive! The words of Gamaliel came back to mind and I experienced the truth of them now. Yes, this Jesus and the movement of the Nazarenes were of God. Gamaliel's words had been prophetic. "But if it is from God, you will not be able to overthrow them. You may even find yourselves fighting against God!" I had been contending with God, which was not a winning proposition.

What a transformation was taking place in me! I remembered the Stoics' belief that moderation was the salvation of humanity. The idea of the Stoics on moderation was so inadequate to save sinful humanity. However, there was something of merit in the Stoic thought on moderation. It reflected the mindset of one who is a servant of Jesus Christ. Through a life of moderation, a believer shows others the presence of Jesus at hand in one's life. Moderation reflects the depths of faith through a relationship with Jesus by finding salvation, joy and peace, and an eternal relationship with Jehovah from one's Core Being.

With all my blind zeal drained, with God's peace ruling my heart, I was able to display humble moderation and consideration for others because the salvation of humanity came through Jesus the Messiah who provided Himself as the means for a true relationship with God. My zeal against the belief that Jesus was Messiah was a product of my pride. My humility came from the example of Jesus who showed by His life that any who follow Him find peace with God.

Educated in Solitude

Over the next few weeks, my zeal transformed into unashamedly preaching Jesus Christ crucified for our sin and raised again because His redemptive work was complete. The Holy Spirit spoke through my Core being with the gifts from my Creator. My fellow Hellenized Jews would challenge me, but the Holy Spirit guided my speech with moderation and humility.

The Holy Spirit directed me to go to Arabia for three years where I was tutored by the Spirit of the risen Christ. Remember, I had very little knowledge of Jesus of Nazareth until I met a Nazarene. Stephen's discourse acquainted me with the belief that this Jesus of Nazareth was the Messiah. I learned how He came in human form by virgin birth with the plan to die for sin to bring us to God.

At the end of three years, the Spirit of God led me to back to Damascus. As I shared in the synagogue, the Spirit of the risen Christ empowered me to give clear defense that Jesus of Nazareth was Messiah. A group of Damascene Jews waited in the city gates planning to kill me. Believers in Damascus heard of the plot and helped me escape by lowering me in a basket over the city wall out of sight of the gates.

I went to Jerusalem to meet with the Apostles who refused to see me thinking I was tricking them to capture them. They were afraid based on my past reputation for searching Jerusalem to find the Nazarenes. When I met and became acquainted with Barnabas, he approached the Apostles on my behalf assuring them that my conversion was genuine. For a brief time, I went with the Apostles to synagogues in Jerusalem and bore witness to my encounter with the living Christ. In a synagogue with Hellenized Jews, I was drawn into debate regarding the person of Jesus as Christ, the Anointed of God. I spoke what I had learned from the Holy Spirit in the custom of Greek debate. When the Hellenized Jews could not win their point, they attempted to kill me. The believers of Jerusalem escorted me to Caesarea and put me aboard a ship bound for Tarsus for my safety.

The days at sea were a time of reflection on all that had transpired in the eight years since sailing to Jerusalem. As we sailed into the harbor, the vista was an amazing demonstration of the beauty of the Creator's handiwork. What my eyes beheld were the Tarsian harbor in the foreground, the city of Tarsus behind, and the backdrop of the blue hues of the white-capped Tarsus Mountains. My vision of home was heartwarming. I returned to my family home where I greeted my father and mother. I began each day in meditation and prayer then went to the family shop to make tents, sewing the walls and roof panels together according to the orders to be filled. I continued to learn at the feet of resurrected Jesus by His Spirit through His Word.

Called to Active Service

After four years of meditation, prayer, and sewing tents, I heard a shout from the Agora. "Saul, grace and peace to you through our Lord Jesus Christ." I recognized the voice and looked for Barnabas. Our embrace was heartwarming for me. Barnabas was so excited to share his news that he could not restrain himself. "Saul, I have come from Antioch to find and fetch you." Barnabas, ever the encourager, told the mighty work the Holy Spirit was doing in Antioch. Many of the Jews there had turned to Christ. However, to Barnabas, the real excitement was the multitudes of Gentiles accepting Jesus as the Son of God who loved them and died for them.

"That is why I am here Saul. The believers in Jerusalem sent me to Antioch for the sake of the Gospel. I was only there for a short time and began to see the immensity of the work. I knew from the Lord that I had to find you to work with me at Antioch. I immediately came to find you. You must return with me."

Hearing of the Spirit of God so mightily at work among the Gentiles of Antioch, I could not contain my excitement. My prayer over the past four years was that God use me to glorify Himself. The opportunity had arrived. My desire to serve the risen Christ was evident in my answer as I voiced a resounding "Yes." After a hearty meal, packing for the journey, and a good night's rest, Barnabas and I set out for Antioch.

In ten years time, I had encountered the risen Christ and I had personally accepted the Good News that Jesus suffered, died, and rose again completing the atonement for the sin of all humanity. This was and is the Gospel of Jesus Christ, the message of the Good News that was to the Jew first and then to the Gentile. In my social contacts with fellow Jews, I went by the name Saul and spoke Hebrew. In my relationships with the Gentiles, I went by my Greco-Roman name, Paul and spoke Koine Greek. My Core identity Saul Paulus was how the Creator knew me. Not just Jew and not just Gentile but made whole by the transforming power of God, Saul Paulus, a servant of Jesus Christ.

I, Saul, have related my story to this point as a Hellenized Jew, a Pharisee, a Zealot for the Torah and Jehovah's Law. At this point, my story changes because I began to speak primarily to Gentiles in Koine Greek using the Septuagint, the Greek translation of the Tanakh that included the Torah or Teachings, the Prophets, and the Writings. The Gentiles who I served for the sake of the Gospel called me Paul.

My encounter with the risen Messiah had changed me. I had served God by keeping His Law. What my Creator really wanted me to do was to serve Him first through a personal relationship with Him then to share the message of the Gospel. I want to share with you how God used my experiences growing up in Tarsus to serve the Gospel of Jesus Christ to the Gentiles.

The Pedagogic Servant

When I left Tarsus for Jerusalem and my education as a lawyer, I was a Pharisee already. Serving the Law of God was what I considered my calling. I had rationalized in my spirit that my judgments were fair and reasonable for righteousness sake. I could get pretty high and mighty in thought and action as was evident in my zealousness against the Nazarenes. Through the Holy Spirit, I learned that true righteousness only came through faith, because no one could live up to God's Law. I ponder Father Abraham with whom God was pleased. Abraham did not know God's Law but God considered him righteous and was pleased with him. I thought further about faith versus keeping the Law.

The Holy Spirit brought to mind the learned slave who was responsible to teach the Nobleman's son in Tarsus. The son was put under the tutor's instruction and until his instruction was complete, the heir had no status. The tutor or pedagogue owned him. To the Nobleman, the slave who was the heir's pedagogue had more status than the heir. When the day came that the pedagogue had finished his job, the son was made an heir once again.

Mulling over a number of ideas, I realized that God's Law was my pedagogue. Until I came into spiritual maturity, I was a slave under the Law, my pedagogue. I who should rightly be an heir was shown time and again by my pedagogue that I fell short of God's standard of righteousness. The Law as my pedagogue showed me in merciless ways how much I missed the mark that I was to attain. The bar was set so high it was impossible for me to reach that mark.

When I met Jesus of Nazareth, I learned that by faith in Him I was made righteous before God. He became my substitute. The Law could not find fault in Him. He the incarnate Son died in my place. When I came to Jesus by faith believing that He was my substitute, my redemption, my atonement, and my reconciliation, the Law had finished its job. My pedagogue, the Law, taught me well that I could not attain to God's righteous standard. Rather than remain in my pompous Pharisaic denial or wither in hopelessness unable to please God, I found faith in Jesus Christ; the suffering Messiah set me free from the condemnation of the Law, my pedagogue.

I met a group of young believers in the country of Galatia north of Cilicia who despaired of ever being able to please God. These Gentiles were being taught that they had to keep the Law of God even after salvation. I helped them learn that salvation did not come from obedience to God's Law but from faith in Jesus Christ. I shared many things to bolster their faith through Jesus Christ. One was the indicator that their salvation was true. I showed them what I had learned from the Holy Spirit. When the Spirit of God indwells us, our faith in Jesus transforms the sinner into a saint. The evidence of the Spirit's presence is the behaviors of love, joy, peace, patience, kindness, goodness, faithfulness, gentleness, and self-control. The Law cannot produce these. They are the product of faith in Jesus Christ within the Believer from the presence of His Indwelling Spirit.

The Emptied Servant

I, Paul, as a servant to the Gospel can find no better example to follow than that of the person of Jesus Christ. I sought to be an example to the Believers I met in Philippi. Lydia was one of the first to accept the Gospel of Jesus Christ. When we were going to look for lodging that night, Lydia insisted that our whole company come to her house. When we refused, she said, "Is my conversion real? Then you must accept my hospitality as confirmation of my faith." Lydia was a willing servant with the gift of hospitality. I wanted those in Philippi to know service based on the example of Jesus as Messiah.

Jesus, the Son of God, shared equally the qualities of Jehovah, as did the Father and the Spirit. When the time came, He willingly relinquished His divine privilege and entered this material world. Jesus, God in human flesh, was limited by time and space. Born of the seed of woman, He fulfilled Jehovah's promise to the Serpent of what would be his demise. He fulfilled the promise to Adam and Eve of the reconciliation of humanity to Jehovah.

He further humbled Himself by becoming obedient to the Father as evident in His actual death that was necessary to atone for humanity's sin and to reconcile humanity's hostility. He who was righteous, not guilty of any sin, died a criminal's death of capital punishment on a cross. Jesus Christ in His deity had the right to call a legion of angels to rescue Him from the Cross. The Hosts of Heaven's Army listened for His command for rescue that never came.

As a faithful servant, Jesus Christ chose to look beyond the Cross and the Grave to the outcome. He anticipated joy as the result of His suffering. His resurrection was accomplished because He had finished His service for salvation. Once He had atoned for all of humanity's sin, He was raised to life because the work was complete. He ascended into the Father's presence with great celebration because He brought a myriad of alienated prodigals home. The Father rewarded Him with a name and an exalted place that every knee of every individual, authority, being, force, and power in all of Creation will bend in His presence. All creation must honor and exalt Him, giving Him the acknowledgement and praise that He rightly deserves. The Creator's grief over the loss of humanity to sin could finally end.

Anyone who sees and accepts that Jesus as the suffering Servant died, was buried, and rose again has taken the steps of faith required. The result of His service to you and me as believers is cleansing, forgiveness, and reconciliation. The natural result that follows that belief is a Core desire to serve Him in return. That service is easy to give out of the gratitude of our hearts for His great Love that He has shown to us.

✍ *Journal Time — How Have You Experienced The Mind of Christ?*

The Irony of God's Timing

Irony had its place in Greek philosophy. Socrates the Greek scholar used it to provoke thought in his listeners by making statements that contained opposites. I used one in speaking to the Corinthians when I described the power of the Gospel of Jesus Christ. In that approach, the listener was brought to an understanding of something incomprehensible in human logic.

Jesus came into this world with the prime purpose to die to atone for sin. He demonstrated his power as the Son of God in healing the sick, in feeding the multitudes, in turning water to wine, in stilling the raging storm, and so on. He taught using the Tanakh—the Teachings, the Prophets, and the Writings. He established clearly what the kingdom of God entailed. In the Creator's plan, He sent His Son to this world, in human flesh to live a holy life and die. He chose a historical time of the most gruesome capital punishment ever. His criteria was that His Son must die displayed before the whole world in the most degrading, shameful way unjustly accused of sin in order for humanity to be reconciled.

Human law had to condemn Him though He was innocent. The Jewish Court condemned Him for blasphemy, for claiming to be Messiah God though His life proved Him such. The Roman Court condemned Him for insurrection because He claimed to be the King of the Jews by the witness of the Jewish people. He was crucified instead of a state criminal Barabbas who was pardoned and released in spite of his most heinous antisocial crimes before both Jew and Gentile societies.

Jesus was judged guilty before Jewish and Roman Courts. He was humiliated with tauntings and beatings, adorned with a robe and a mock crown made from a wreath of thorns; He bore His own cross to Calvary outside of Jerusalem. His hands and feet were nailed to the cross that was raised to hang publicly in full view of passing humanity as the demonstration of His guilt and shame. His side was pierced to speed His death. His charges were posted over His head for all to read—This is Jesus, King of the Jews.

The Creator had planned this before the footings of the edifice of the Universe were laid down. All this was done to reconcile humanity alienated by Adam's sin. Adam disobeyed the Creator in the Garden of Eden by eating the fruit of the Wisdom Tree that gave the knowledge of good and evil. As a servant to the Gospel of Jesus Christ, I proclaimed a message that is foolish, ridiculous, to some even insane. Why? Because this humanly implausible message is the means of reconciliation for humanity to return to a relationship with the Creator. It is the atoning power of God whose love was demonstrated through the sacrifice of His own Son to anyone who will accept it.

Irony—The preaching of the Cross is to those who are perishing—foolishness! But to you and me who believe, it is the power of God that brought us salvation.

Irony—God loved us in spite of our attitude of hostility toward Him. He by the death of His Son did what was necessary to provide the means of restoration for us to have a relationship with Him.

The Creator's timing demonstrates such amazing patience. To make promises and then to wait patiently for the right moment to make good on those promises is from human logic incredulous. He waited until that moment in human history when the worst form of death existed that would cover every prophecy made for atonement to be accomplished.

The translation of Moses and the Prophets into Greek, the universal language of the world, happened shortly before Jesus' birth. My birth was 5 years after Jesus was born. I was born a Jew in another country because of our nation's unfaithfulness to Jehovah. I was raised with the Law of God on my lips and in my heart because of my family's desire to follow Jehovah. I was born with both Jewish and Roman citizenship. I could speak, read, and write both Hebrew and Greek. I was socialized as a Jew from birth. My naturalized Roman citizenship from birth led to my acculturation as a Gentile. My father and grandfather taught me a trade. But I elected to go to Jerusalem to receive my education in Mosaic Law and to become a member of the Great Sanhedrin. I knew nothing of Jesus though He was my contemporary; I heard of Him after His death through the problem of the Nazarene cult in Jerusalem. When I met Him on the road to Damascus, He taught me by His Spirit who He was and why He came to die. After my conversion, my education by the Holy Spirit was in the solitude of Arabia for three years beyond human influence. The Spirit of the resurrected Jesus Christ continued to teach and prepare me to be a servant of His Gospel. Then the Holy Spirit's call to serve the Gospel of Jesus Christ came through Barnabas to go to Antioch.

As I look back over my life, I see how the Creator prepared me in my Core being to become His servant. He used my experiences in life as resources to draw from for the sake of the Gospel. While my experience was for a time and place as a contemporary of Jesus' Apostles, every believer can follow my example and trust that the Holy Spirit will guide you to the Creator's plan for your life of service to the Gospel of the risen Christ.

Irony—I, Paul, became an Apostle of Jesus Christ though I was born at the wrong time and place. To qualify as an Apostle of Jesus Christ, one had to see Jesus alive after His resurrection and see Him ascended to Glory. As disciples first, the Apostles walked with Him for three years before His death and then saw Him raised alive and glorified. I saw Him alive, glorified, and then walked with Him for three years learning from Him through His Spirit. He prepared me uniquely to serve Him by spreading the Good News to the Gentiles.

The Creator's plan for every believer is as unique as the Core identity He gave to each of us. He endowed each of us with life, identity, talents, and direction through His Spirit that through our existence, we will serve and praise Him with the whole of our Core being. Part of our service is to share the Gospel of Christ with others.

Irony — Another ironic part of my story is how Roman citizenship provided me the greatest opportunity for service. In Philippi, while sharing the message of Christ, a woman being trafficked by Macedonians as a fortuneteller saw Silas and me and loudly proclaimed, "These men are servants of the Most High God, and they have come to tell you how to be saved." She did this day after day until I became annoyed and commanded the spirit of the world to leave her. Her handlers became outraged because she no longer had the abilities to earn them so much money.

They dragged Silas and me to the town square where the officials of Philippi had the makings of a full-scale riot on their hands. To appease the handlers and the citizens siding with them, the city officials had us beaten and imprisoned. Silas and I praised Jehovah, singing into the night locked in stocks in the deepest part of the jail. An earthquake broke all the cell doors open. The jailer on seeing the cells open was about to commit suicide. I called out assuring him that every prisoner was present. Having heard Silas and me rejoicing in spite of our severe beatings, he asked to accept Christ as his Savior. Our suffering had a wonderful outcome; the jailer and his family accepted the Gospel.

The next morning the city officials sent the police officer to tell the jailer to release us now that the potential for a riot was passed. I refused to be released and told the police officer to report to the city council that Silas and I were Roman citizens and that our right to a fair trial was not allowed. The city officials came to the jail to escort us out announcing to the people of Philippi that we, by birth Roman citizens, were treated wrongly. They made a public apology and released us. They wanted us to leave town quickly; but, asserting our rights, we went to Lydia's house and met with the believers in Philippi to encourage them in faith; then we departed.

One of the last times I was in Jerusalem, Jews from Asia accosted in the Temple and falsely accused me of breaking God's Law. I was interred at the Fortress for Roman soldiers. I attempted to make my defense before the High Council in the Temple court while guarded by Roman soldiers since I was a Roman citizen. The Roman garrison commander tried for two days to sort out why I was at the center of such dissension. I did not get off to a good start when my words were an offense to Ananias the high priest that I did not know. I apologized and quoted the scripture, "You must not speak evil of any of your rulers." Then I went on to say, "Brothers, I am a Pharisee, as were my ancestors! And I am on trial because my hope is in the resurrection of the dead." The result was the Pharisees and the Sadducees, who disagreed about the resurrection of the dead, began arguing amongst themselves. The Roman Garrison leader returned me to the Fortress for safety.

That night my nephew overheard forty men taking a vow not to eat until they killed me in ambush on the way to court the next day. My nephew came to the Fortress and shared what he overheard. I directed him to go to the Garrison commander and tell him. As a result, the Garrison commander privately arranged that at the ninth hour that evening four hundred seventy soldiers were to escort me to Caesarea in protective custody. He brought a letter of introduction to Governor Felix who would keep me in prison at Herod's Headquarters for the next two years.

I was allowed to present my defense before a number of Roman leaders because I was a Roman citizen by birth. I insisted on my right to present my defense before Caesar. The persistence of the Jewish leadership to cause my death, my asserting my rights as a Roman citizen for a fair trial, being heard by regional Governors and kings, and finally my appeal to appear before Caesar allowed me to share the Gospel of Jesus Christ with many world leaders in a five year period of time. After I was released from prison in Rome, I travelled for the Gospel's sake for another three years and then returned to Rome.

Irony—My status as a Roman Citizen by birth protected me extending my life so I could continue my service to the Gospel of

Jesus Christ. In those times I was able to bring the message of the Gospel before world leaders. All that I did was through the power of the Spirit of the risen Jesus.

The Mind of the True Servant

I wrote these words to reflect what I was learning and experiencing as a servant of Jesus Christ.

Intentional Rejoicing—"Always be full of joy in the Lord. I say it again, rejoice!"

Humble Moderation – "Let everyone see that you are considerate in all you do. Remember, the Lord is coming soon."

Expressive Trust – "Don't worry about anything; instead, pray about everything. Tell God what you need, and thank him for all he has done."

Incomprehensible Peace – "Then you will experience God's peace, which exceeds anything we can understand. His peace will guard your hearts and minds as you live in Christ Jesus."

Mindful Focus – "Fix your thoughts on what is true, and honorable, and right, and pure, and lovely, and admirable. Think about things that are excellent and worthy of praise."

New Habits – "Keep putting into practice all you learned and received from me, everything you heard from me and saw me doing."

Eternal Presence – "Then the God of peace will be with you."

The experiences encapsulated in these seven phrases are the summary of the transformation of my mind and thoughts from the Core of my being.

I wrote out these verses when I shared Christ as an example of a servant with the Christians of Philippi. I wanted them to be reassured that as a servant of Jesus there may be difficulties, but we are not alone in the struggles. I wanted to encourage them to see that being a servant of Jesus from one's Core being is a privilege. So in a letter to them I wrote the following:

"For you have been given not only the privilege of trusting in Christ but also the privilege of suffering for him. We are in this struggle together. You have seen my struggle in the past, and you know that I am still in the midst of it." (I wanted them to identify with the truth that in suffering as a servant of the Gospel – We are not alone!)

- Is there any encouragement from belonging to Christ?
- Is there any comfort from His love?
- Is there any fellowship with others through the Spirit?
- Are your hearts tender and compassionate?"

I asked these questions to make the Philippians mindful that the relationship with Christ provides us encouragement and comfort from a support system with others who are like-minded. I also wanted them to realize that our hearts have been softened and we have the capacity for sympathy and empathy as Christ did.

With that realization of the transformation that comes as a result of a relationship with Christ, I asked that the Philippians reflect that change in the manner by how they related to one another. I could be truly happy to know through their actions that I had successfully served Christ and the Gospel.

- Agree wholeheartedly with each other,
- Love one another,
- Work together with one mind and purpose.

To add a conscious element to the transformation within them, I encouraged them to stay mindful of the new habits they were developing. The attitude of Jesus Christ was one that they must strive to reflect in their lives.

- Don't be selfish.
- Don't try to impress others.

• Be humble, thinking of others as better than yourselves.
• Don't look out only for your own interests, but take an interest in others, too.

I left a legacy for all those at Philippi that they were to pass on. I taught by fatherly example. I lived out the example of Jesus so they had a tangible experience of what that was to be like.

✍ *Journal Time—What Can You Do to Be More Committed in Service?*

A True Servant Trains His Replacement

I had a sense that my end of service on Earth was drawing near. I went back in my mind to the Grecian games to take inventory of my life. I purposefully practiced physical discipline so my body was fit for service. In reflecting on my life circumstances, I can see how I survived through tough situations by God's grace.

One time I was stoned by fellow Pharisees and left for dead outside Lystra. I was beaten at five different cities. I was shipwrecked a number of times. I fought wild animals in the coliseum at Ephesus. I share these experiences with you neither to get pity nor to get credit. These events were opportunities to suffer as a servant of Jesus for the Gospel of Christ. My reason for sharing this is to encourage you that if you should suffer for the Gospel of Christ, He will empower you to live and endure. Just remain true in your faith. Remember by His death and resurrection, He removed the sting of death.

I want you to know that all those who died before us are those who sit in the grandstands at the finish line and are cheering us on. When I wrote of the cloud of witnesses, I referred to men and women of faith who believed God's promise and lived accordingly. God appraised their faith as righteous. Enoch, Noah, Abraham, Sarah, Isaac, Jacob, are just a few of the myriad of witnesses who by faith pleased God. I encourage you to be mindful of those and to stay faithful as you run your race in service to Jehovah.

I wept for the Galatians who had become confused by those who preached a gospel other than the Gospel of Christ. They were being told that they had to obey the Mosaic Law first. I hoped that they would stay the course and that God would reveal to them the lies of these false teachers. I reminded them that God through Christ has set them free from the law. The law who was our pedagogue had completed its teaching duties because Jesus Christ had come and fulfilled the law. Through Jesus, they had matured beyond the lessons of the pedagogue.

To my friends at Philippi, I encouraged them to hold the word of life with a firm grip. I told them as I awaited the end of my life I knew that they would be the evidence that my servanthood was of value. I kept striving for holiness as Christ had made it possible. I did not look to my failures of the past but kept my focus on the end of the race.

At the end of the race, the Greek athletes approached the raised platform, the "Bema," where the runner was judged and rewards were given. If he did not come in first, but did finish the race, the runner would bow before the race official who would give the proper reward. The winner of the race bowed to have the Victor's Crown placed upon his head.

I look forward to standing on the Bema before Jesus, the Anointed One, and receive from His hand my reward for finishing the race as His faithful servant. I can picture myself bowing my head before Him as He places the Crown of Righteousness on my head. Remember, I told the Philippians that I was not perfect nor had I attained perfection in life. I do know however that in Christ I am perfect. He became my righteousness to bring me to God.

My thoughts went to Timothy, my son in the faith. As I shared my awareness that the time of my death was near, I could say to him:

> I have fought the good fight, I have finished the race, and I have remained faithful. And now the prize awaits me—the crown of righteousness, which the Lord, the righteous Judge, will give me on the day of his return. And the prize is not just for me but for all who eagerly look forward to His return." (1 Timothy 4:7-8 NLT)

To Timothy and the many I had trained and encouraged in the faith, I could say–"Be an example of me as I am of Christ." because of Jesus who was my example for service.

My wish for you is the same; as I shared with other believers—"Don't conform to how others think and act, don't just take the easy way out. Let God transform your mind and your thoughts to serve and please Him. Practice that way of thinking until it becomes second nature to you. Then you too will have the mind of Christ."

✍ *Journal Time—How Does Paul's Narrative Encourage You to Serve?*

Chapter 3

THE FIRST CORE EXPRESSION—SERVICE

What Motivated the Good Samaritan?

> "Pure and genuine religion in the sight of God the Father means caring for orphans and widows in their distress and refusing to let the world corrupt you." (James 1:27 NLT)

The Creator made all humanity in His image designed for His purpose. Service to one another is one aspect of the Creator's design. A spiritual relationship with God by means of the work of Christ on the cross is not the basis by which humanity serves. The Creator is a relational God and service is a means for humanity to build relationships. Anyone can serve even if the individual does not have a personal relationship with God. However, one who has a relationship with Christ will serve beyond the natural ability general to humanity. It is my hope that as you think on the Core expression of service you are amazed at the Creator's design. This important feature of His plan counted on the Core expression of service to build unity and community.

Because of the Creator's handiwork, any human being has the capacity to do good works. The Apostle James, ever the one to cut to the chase in defining human behavior, defines pure and genuine religion as actions that serve the helpless and needy and that represent moral choice. In that last phrase we find the distinction between humanity in general and the individual who desires to honor the Creator by living a holy life.

Social psychologists C. D. Batson and J. M. Darley looked at the story of the Good Samaritan from Luke 10 and pondered the social behaviors of the three individuals who witnessed someone in need.[7] In response to a question, "Who is my neighbor?" Jesus tells the story of a Jewish man, travelling on the road from Jerusalem to Jericho. The Romans likely paved this road for troop transport so it was wide enough to make it ideal for a range of uses. However, a common event of that time was that gangs would hide along the roadside, ambush travellers, and steal their money. The gang who ambushed this traveller violently beat him senseless and took everything he had down to his last stitch of clothing; then they left him for dead. Jesus continues the tale telling of three men who came upon the injured traveller. Each had the opportunity to serve this wounded man.

The first man was a Jewish priest whose role was to offer sacrifices before God in the Temple. When the priest saw his fellow Jew lying bloody and beaten along the road ahead, he crossed over to the opposite side. The next traveller, a Levite, was an assistant who would have worked with the priest at the Temple in the role of preparing for and cleaning up after Temple services. This man saw the injured man, went over to look at him, but continued on his journey. The third man was a Samaritan, one who was of mixed ethnicity of Jewish and Canaanite descent and despised for that.

This individual saw the traveler's suffering, was stirred to compassion, tended to the man's injuries, and put him on his donkey to take the man to an inn farther along the road. The Samaritan took a room at the inn and tended to the man's injuries through the night. In the morning, the Samaritan arranged with the innkeeper to cover the expense of the injured man's lodging until he healed. At the end of the story, Jesus asked a question of his audience, "Which of the three men was the injured man's neighbor?" Only the Samaritan, a social outcast, actively demonstrated Core traits of service and compassion through his actions.

Batson and Darley were interested in what motivated the prosocial behaviors of serving others. They had three hypotheses:

1. People thinking religious or "helping" thoughts would still be no more likely than others to offer assistance.
2. People in a hurry will be less likely to offer aid.
3. People who are religious in a Samaritan manner will be more likely to help than those with a priest or Levite mindset.

In other words, people who are religious for what it will gain them will be less likely to help than those who value religion for the sake of spiritual significance.

Batson and Darley asked seminary students to prepare a sermon on the story of the Good Samaritan. The seminary students were only aware that they were participating in research on religious education. On the day of the experiment, the students arrived at the research center with their sermons ready. The students took tests and surveys that would provide relevant information on each of them.

On completing the assessment, each student received one of three sets of instructions assigned randomly by the researchers. The instructions given to each participant were worded in such a way to create a degree of urgency: to make the student feel highly hurried, medium hurried, or low hurried as he went to the next building to deliver his sermon. Each seminary student walked independently through an alley on his way to the second building. A man sat slumped in an alley doorway. As each one passed, the man moaned and coughed twice.

Arriving at the next building, each student gave his talk and then answered another questionnaire. What do you think were Batson and Darley's conclusions? Each seminarian had been studying the story of the Good Samaritan in preparation for his sermon. Did the sermon topic sensitize each to reach out to help the man in the doorway?

The answer from this research showed how the degree of hurriedness influenced how each student responded to the man in trouble. The results overall were that 43% offered help to the man. Of the low hurried group, 63% helped; of the medium hurried group, 45% helped; and of the high hurried group, 10% helped. If a seminarian saw religion as a duty, he was less likely to help the man in the alley.

Batson and Darley drew two conclusions: that the level of hurriedness had an influence on whether help was given to a person in need and that a mindset of duty reduced prosocial behavior.

Reflecting back on the three men in the parable of the Good Samaritan, was the priest in a hurry to get to the next Temple sacrifice to officiate and for that reason he ignored the injured man? At least the Temple assistant looked; but was there urgency for him to go on to his job? Did that mean that the Samaritan was a laid-back person with time and money available to tend to the injured man? The researchers were not discrediting the parable of Jesus, but thinking about what the motives of each traveler might have been.

Why Do People Serve?

Social research paid much attention to the source of antisocial behavior and its effect on society. Antisocial behavior, usually criminal in nature, attacks the underpinnings of social structure and security. Victims of antisocial behavior lose safety and trust and incur expenses from medical and psychological care to heal the injury. Society accrues other expenses to maintain law and order, to fund jurisprudence, and to maintain a penal system to protect society from criminality.

C. D. Batson was interested in the study of prosocial behavior, those actions intended to help or to serve others.[8] He concluded the following motivations relate to prosocial behavior. We will explore these ideas as related to our model that contrasts Core identity with Relational identity. Take note of which motivations originate from within one's Core being without regard for what others may think. Let's work with the same set of problems that Batson used to more easily understand each motivation.

Batson's Premise: A person stirred to serve from scenes on the news like the plight of hurricane victims, the lack of food and shelter for homeless children, or wanton vandalism to community buildings, parks, or cemeteries does so for these reasons:

<u>Self-serving benefit</u>—One person volunteers for a Big Brother or Big Sister program to mentor teens and reduce adolescent crime so that others see him or her as a civic minded person. This is one way to define one's Relational identity and have others know you as you wish to be known. Volunteerism also looks good on job resumes.

Undoing the Past—Service can provide relief to a person haunted by social wrongs committed in one's adolescence. A businessman recognized as one who is community minded leads a team to clean up graffiti on public buildings. Each time he sees graffiti, a surge of shame and guilt rises within him over things he and his friends did as teenagers without consequences. In an attempt to quiet his emotions, he serves to make retribution to his community for his secret wrongs. His hope is that his actions will finally quiet his emotional turmoil.

Staying Busy to Avoid—Service can provide a person with enough activity to avoid a soul-searching look at one's own life. A woman joins a relief effort for hurricane survivors. She keeps busy contacting local suppliers of packaged foods, personal items, and clothing donations to be shipped by semi transport to the disaster area. In her busyness, she does not have to think about her loved one who just died. Her activity pushes away her feelings of grief and loss. When the current project is over, she may be faced with what she avoided or may throw herself into another project to continue to avoid her feelings of grief.

Demonstrating Responsibility—A person might hold a position in a community organization out of a sense of social duty or to prove he is a responsible person. Prior criticism that he never stuck to anything led to the determination for one man to prove to his friends, neighbors, and family that he could be counted on. He attended every meeting of a social action committee that was planning a homeless shelter. He had no money to give to the cause but he gave of his time and ability as a handyman. His determination was to show others of his community that he could stick to something and that he was dependable.

Showing Social Conscience—Individuals see news images of the various social woes and feel a genuine empathy for the suffering of others. Individuals are stirred to act out of Core compassion and seek to participate in what will alleviate suffering not simply for one person but for the greater good of the human race. The Core identity of such a person seeks to serve others as a natural expression of love for one's neighbor. Batson calls this behavior "Empathic Altruism." Empathy is the ability to recognize the feelings of others, to be able to be in another person's shoes, and to show compassion for others who are suffering. Altruism is a belief or practice one holds out of concern for the welfare of society as a whole. This is the world's explanation of why people do acts of kindness.

Showing the Mind of Christ—A personal relationship with Jesus Christ introduces a motivation that is not in Batson's list. Any individual who accepts the redeeming work of Christ wants his or her life to reflect an intimate relationship with the Creator through service. Paul described the attitude Jesus took when He chose to serve humanity through His death. The letter Paul wrote to the church at Philippi describes the extent to which Jesus went so that we could be reconciled to a Holy God. Jesus, as our Creator, was motivated not by empathic altruism but by obedience to His Father. Jesus looked beyond the suffering He was to face, knowing that His obedience to the Will of His Father would result in joy. Paul encourages us to be motivated like Jesus and serve out of obedience and in faith look to the future joy of being with Him in eternity. This form of service seeks to express gratitude to the Creator for His salvation.

Reflect for a moment on serving someone in need. What thoughts and feelings did you encounter? Which of the above motivations were your reasons for serving? Motivations other than the last two in the list lead to serving from your Relational self. To serve from social conscience is a Core expression of the unbeliever because of the hard-wiring of the Creator in humanity. To serve out of gratitude in light of all that Jesus has done for you is the natural Core response of the believer.

Is sharing the Gospel of Jesus Christ with others empathic altruism or is it much deeper? Sharing the message of salvation is an important service that honors God. When you look at how Paul shared the message of Christ, you will find that he considered his audience. When he was in the Temple or a synagogue, he reminded his Jewish audience what the Tanakh taught about the Messiah. He shared that the prophets had said the Messiah would suffer and die for Israel. He pointed to the contemporary signs that proved Jesus Christ was in truth the promised Messiah. When Paul met with Gentiles, he appealed to reason with powerful logic. He showed how this man Jesus was the unknown God they sought. Paul by the Holy Spirit brought Gentiles to a sense of wonderment that the Eternal God came into this world to die for the sinner rather than destroy the sinner.

When he met with the Jews and Gentiles who believed in Jesus, he taught them how to follow Christ and live for Him. The spread of Christianity happened as believers in a community would invite others to hear Paul and those with him tell the message of salvation. As a believer grew in faith and the knowledge of Jesus, he or she would boldly share with others and invite them into the kingdom of God. Even the common townspeople heard the message of Christ as Paul appeared before the local authorities accused of civil disobedience. As a natural born Roman citizen, Paul used his rights to free speech and a fair trial to publicly proclaim the Gospel. The result was people coming to saving faith and the early church grew exponentially.

Paul would unashamedly speak guided by the Spirit of God in a manner that would reach out to the people of that culture. Paul's Jewish and Grecian heritage gave him a cross-cultural understanding that the Holy Spirit used to bring people to Christ. He served the local believers by establishing churches and leaving them under the spiritual leadership of men and women like Timothy, Titus, Luke, Lydia, Priscilla, and Aquila.

The narrative of the Apostle Paul, a historical person of the Bible, is a demonstration of the transforming power of an encounter with the risen Christ. The very name that Paul wished to erase from the lips of every person on planet Earth was the one that changed his heart to become the man who took that name, Jesus, before governors, kings, and Emperors. Paul, more than any other human being, was responsible by the Spirit of God for the spread of the Gospel of Jesus Christ. His passion to serve the Law of God was redirected to serve the Gospel of Christ, and to fan the fires of service in every believer. Paul wanted every believer to know that the demonstration of God's love at the expense of Jesus His Son could transform one's life, as it had his own.

Is the desire to serve characteristic of religion and Christianity or might it exist in the secular world as well? I remind you that Core behaviors can manifest in saint and sinner alike for the simple reason that our Creator designed humanity in His image. The Core expression of service is not dependent on faith; it is hard-wired in humanity by original design. However, when any human being accepts the work of reconciliation accomplished through Jesus, the person's Core identity emerges from the dust and ruin caused by Adam's sin to stand boldly before Holy God. By this stage in the *Coming to Awe, Finding Identity* series, I trust that you know the awe of serving the Creator from your Core being as your expression of gratitude for His redeeming love.

How the Brain Relates to Service

You were introduced to the three main processing areas of the brain in the first chapter. The functions of these three areas are quite a metaphor for how some people live a constricted spiritual life. To live only from the brainstem is to barely be alive physically with only basic vital signs evident. In the spiritual parallel, the vital signs are salvation, baptism, and church attendance without verbal or behavioral expression. To live primarily from the limbic or emotional brain is to serve out of reflexive shame or compulsive avoidance concerned for potential judgment or criticism. To live from the cortex or thinking brain is to serve out of logical obedience without much empathy or compassion.

To serve God with our whole mind from our Core being is the desired expression that glorifies the Creator. Our emotional brain assists Core self in recognizing suffering and need in others; our thinking brain creates the plan while listening to the Spirit of God, which is necessary to serve others effectively. Our Core existence provides the energy to carry on through the choices intended by our Core self to glorify the Lord. This integration is evident in a Core attitude of joy, peace, and love expressed while serving.

I wish that I had access to a research facility with the most advanced developments in brain imaging. It would provide me an opportunity to encounter awe as I witnessed Paul's statement at work in the hard-wiring of the brain—"let God transform you into a new person by changing the way you think." The Hubble telescope allows us to observe substance and activity in the distant reaches of the universe and stand amazed. Neurocognitive science has parallel means to look within the brain and observe. To observe activity in the brain related to service and how it restores and shows healthy Core function would be stunning.

Some recent findings parallel Paul's hypothesis. If fear or shame is active in the limbic brain, it becomes difficult for the person's cortex to introduce thoughts that can quiet fear. The perception of a threat and the strength of the feelings disallow the amygdalae to quiet enough to hear truth. If the limbic brain does not relax, the stress state remains dominant; the emotional beliefs become habit. This is evident in people who serve out of shame. When shame is present, the amygdalae are on alert during the act of service. Concerns about acceptance, approval, or control continue to reinforce shame while one is serving.

When the person can quiet the fear and shame by the simplest form of calming like taking intentional deep breaths, the emotional brain becomes quiet. That is the first step in letting God transform the mind. With a state of calmness, the individual can hear reason and truth from the thinking brain. This step teaches of God's character through His Word and builds trust in God's eternal love. When that truth has replaced the shame and fear, then seeing someone in need brings a natural response of service. These are not the reactive emotional thoughts of "Should I help? What will she or others think? Do I have time? She was being clumsy; it serves her right." Core self knows this is an opportunity to show grace to others.

The neurocognitive picture of the areas of the brain that become active in prosocial service shows the individual is serving from the thinking mind. The empathic feelings will be present without a survival state in control. Appreciation shown by the other person reinforces the internal calm that allows the thought of gratitude: "Lord, thank you for the opportunity to serve you." That is how God's transformation works: changed from a person who worries about what others think, to a person who can serve in the moment from the Core self, free to glorify the Creator for who He is.

Research findings in the areas of addictions and obsessive-compulsive disorders are shedding light on how the limbic brain functions in high stress events, how it attempts to regulate activation, and how addictive habits are generated. This research holds out hope to relieve suffering from psychological trauma, substance abuse, and other stress-related problems. How exciting it is to witness the Creator's design physically active within the human mind. Even more so, the Creator designed the human brain to be reset to its original intent where the cortex is executive in processing over the limbic system. The means of that reset is found in Scripture. Truth brings trust, safety, and peace.

Contemplate these verses in light of our discussion. The imagery in these passages speaks truth that will produce calming within the limbic brain.

"Those who love your instructions have great peace and do not stumble." (Psalm 119:165 NLT)

"You will keep in perfect peace all who trust in you, all whose thoughts are fixed on you!" (Isaiah 26:3 NLT)

"And this righteousness will bring peace. Yes, it will bring quietness and confidence…" (Isaiah 32:16-17 NLT)

"Therefore, since we have been made right in God's sight by faith, we have peace with God because of what Jesus Christ our Lord has done for us." (Romans 5:1 NLT)

"And the peace of God, which surpasses all comprehension, will guard your hearts and your minds in Christ Jesus." (Philippians 4:7 NASB)

These verses also provide a strong visual image of what peace looks like as we focus on Christ. The imagery of these verses is a powerful way to bring to the amygdalae a calming picture of the Creator's power at work in our lives. His peace restores trust and calms the overactive limbic brain.

Gifts Differing

"In his grace, God has given us different gifts for doing certain things well." (Romans 12:6 NLT)

Katharine Cook Briggs and Isabel Briggs Myers were mother and daughter who were interested in Carl Jung's theory of personality. As educators they collaborated on the study of personality type. Isabel Briggs Myers created a paper and pencil version of the test called the Myers Briggs Personality Type Indicator used strictly for research until 1975.[9] At that time the test became a means to help people appreciate differences in others, which in essence was accepting the uniqueness of God's creation as observed in another person's Core being. Both mother and daughter wished these ideas would result in understanding how we are different from one another in the hope that it would foster more harmonious relationships. This test became the basis for other assessments of spiritual gifts and team building. Myers noted the verse in Romans 12:6 from the King James Version that said "Having then gifts differing..." and used that phrase to emphasize a positive quality in our differences from others because of the Creator's design. These verses add support to this truth.

"For we are God's masterpiece. He has created us anew in Christ Jesus, so we can do the good things he planned for us long ago." (Ephesians 2:10 NLT)

"God has given each of you a gift from his great variety of spiritual gifts. Use them well to serve one another." (1 Peter 4:10 NLT)

Our Creator who gave us Core identity also gave us abilities, gifts, or talents for use in serving. There are two reasons for serving: first is to demonstrate the transforming power of the Gospel of Jesus Christ. Any believer can share that good news with someone, either by word, by action, or by example. Our second reason for service is to use the gifts we received from the Holy Spirit to minister to one another for the sake of the body of Christ, our faith community.

Paul shows the Triune Creator involved in every aspect of His intent for us to serve Him. The Spirit endows us with gifts for service, the Lord is whom we serve with those gifts, and the Father directs how we are to serve to fulfill His master plan. The result is that every believer serving from his or her Core being expresses praise that glorifies our Creator.

Gifted Service Has Purpose

Here are specific passages that identify different gifts that are used in service for different purposes that ultimately are to the glory of our Creator who made us, who endowed us with identity, and who equipped us to love and serve our Creator and one another.

Service Provides Endurance—"…you have every spiritual gift you need as you eagerly wait for the return of our Lord Jesus Christ." (1 Corinthians 1:7 NLT)

Service Empowers Excellence—"In his grace, God has given us different gifts for doing certain things well." (Romans 12:6 NLT)

Service Provides Support—"A spiritual gift is given to each of us so we can help each other." (1 Corinthians 12:1 NLT)

"God has given each of you a gift from his great variety of spiritual gifts. Use them well to serve one another." (1 Peter 4:10 NLT)

Service Builds Community—"Now these are the gifts Christ gave to the church…to equip God's people to do his work and build up the church, the body of Christ." (Ephesians 4:11-12 NLT)

Gifts Suit Unique Needs

In three of his epistles, Paul addresses service based on the gifts the Holy Spirit endows on believers. Each of the three churches has a unique challenge that the gifts of the Spirit address. Romans is the first epistle where Paul writes to believers in Rome, which is a church uniquely impacted by the Gospel of Jesus Christ. The message of salvation through Christ came to Rome by word of mouth. Those who had fled Paul's persecution shared the Gospel as they moved from Jerusalem to Damascus on through Asia Minor and into Europe. Roman Christians were the first to understand that the message of the Gospel applied to the Jew and Gentile alike. Salvation was based on the Faith of Abraham rather than the Law of Moses. The message of the Good News was relevant to all humanity because Jew and Gentile alike are sinners falling short of God's Righteousness. Thus through the work of Jesus Christ, any who call on Him have salvation without discrimination of ethnicity, gender, or socioeconomic status.

This new church had members representing such diversity of religious traditions from different forms of Judaism and Paganism. The Gospel of Jesus Christ was the unifying factor that the Holy Spirit used to create unity from the diversity. The Spirit's gifts unified the believers in Rome providing a common understanding of truth. In Romans 12:6-9, Paul lists spiritual gifts that will serve that early church so that the truth regarding the Gospel message is preserved.

Prophecy was a gift that made people aware of the mind of God. Unlike in Jewish tradition where a prophet spoke for God directly to the people, the apostles were foremost in proclaiming the Gospel of Jesus Christ, the prophesied suffering Messiah. The apostles had learned the mind of God from their time as the disciples of Jesus. The gift of prophecy supported the message of the Gospel, bringing knowledge, comfort, and encouragement to those who believed in Jesus. The prophetic gift in believers who were truly humble brought harmony between Jew and Gentile alike in the common faith in the resurrected Christ.

The general attitude toward Christians in Rome was hatred. Remember the socioeconomic conditions that faced the church in Rome in the time of Paul. The members of the church consisted of slaves to the wealthy; impoverished freemen who had been slaves freed because of their faithfulness; and wealthy patrician women who had been Jewish proselytes. These people heard the Gospel of Jesus Christ and accepted the message of salvation. Prophecy as a spiritual gift taught the message of the Gospel, comforted the downtrodden, and encouraged believers to stand firm in their faith against the cultural hatred. Roman Emperors were quick to blame the Christians for any struggles the people of Rome encountered. Prophecy required humble people willing to take a stand for truth to uplift the believers in the face of such animosity.

Other gifts pertinent to the early church worked to create unity and solidarity among believers. Serving was the gift used to minister in practical ways to people who had grave needs in sustaining their health, safety, and welfare. <u>Teaching</u> provided the foundational knowledge of the Gospel of Jesus Christ and taught one to grow and live out their newfound faith. <u>Exhortation</u> provided comfort and encouragement to those who struggled with the loss of loved ones subjected to the violence of the Coliseum. <u>Giving</u> provided those who desired to share in material ways to care for the church and its members. <u>Leadership</u> was the gift that provided unity to this diverse body, directing members' attention to the Person of Christ and the unified fellowship of believers. <u>Showing mercy</u> was a gift crucial to those who suffered for the Gospel, struggled to understand and accept the Gospel, were alienated because of their faith, or were in need of physical help to be able to survive. The church at Rome found unity in Christ and stood up to the adversity that confronted them by these gifts of the Spirit at work in their midst.

The second epistle in which Paul shared teaching on the gifts of the Spirit was to the church at Corinth. This church did not have the adversity as Rome. Jews, Greeks, and Romans had become Christians through Paul's ministry. As time passed, the members were divisively aligning with different spiritual leaders and practices. Each member was functioning from his or her Relational self by showing allegiance to a human leader rather than from Core submission to Christ with a spirit of humility. They tolerated open immorality by one of the church members rather than to taking a courageous stand against it. Arrogance was a predominant trait among many.

> "Here are some of the parts God has appointed for the church: first are apostles, second are prophets, third are teachers, then those who do miracles, those who have the gift of healing, those who can help others, those who have the gift of leadership, those who speak in unknown languages...So you should earnestly desire the most helpful gifts." (1 Corinthians 12:28, 31 NLT)

Paul used the analogy of the human body that is dependent on every part of its physiology to function. No single part of human physiology can claim to be more important than any other part. Paul acknowledged how the Holy Spirit used him and Apollos for a unifying purpose to serve the Gospel of Christ. Neither was more important than the other when it came to the Gospel. The list of gifts that Paul identified for the believers in Corinth identified three gifts crucial for leadership—apostles, prophets, and teachers. The remaining ones were miracles, healing, helps, administration, and unknown languages, all to serve the body of Christ, the church. Paul challenged the church in Corinth to seek and use gifts that benefited all believers and that promoted unity.

Paul's third epistle in which he discussed spiritual gifts was to the church at Ephesus. This church was one made up of a large group of Greeks and Romans. Ephesus was one of the major centers of pagan worship and sexual perversion in the world at that time. The Temple of Diana, a fertility goddess, was a site of wealthy enterprise in human trafficking, sensual fetishes, and magic charms. When the people of Ephesus heard the Gospel and turned to Christ, there were bonfires throughout the city as people burned their books of magic, their idols, and their fetishes. The believers in Ephesus learned from Paul how to live the Christian life each day in practical ways. The depth of their conversion to Christ empowered by Paul's teaching taught them respect for fellow believers and how to stand firm against the forces of darkness in this world.

The message of the Gospel of Christ is unity and peace. There is one Spirit that unifies believers—one Lord, one Faith, one Baptism, one God, and Father who is Lord of all humanity. By the gift of grace through Jesus Christ, we are able to grow into maturity and become like Christ. To accomplish that maturity, each church member is equipped through gifted leadership to serve from his or her Core ability.

> "Now these are the gifts Christ gave to the church: the apostles, the prophets, the evangelists, and the pastors and teachers. Their responsibility is to equip God's people to do his work and build up the church, the body of Christ. This will continue until we all come to such unity in our faith and knowledge of God's Son that we will be mature in the Lord, measuring up to the full and complete standard of Christ." (Ephesians 4:11-13 NLT)

The equipping of God's people means preparing them to use their Core gifts with maturity as Christ desired. The five leadership gifts are designated by the grace of Jesus Christ to prepare the remaining members of the body of Christ to serve the church and one another in love. While Paul's letter to the Ephesians does not discuss specific gifts for each believer, the analogy is that the foundational gifts of apostles, prophets, evangelists, pastors, and teachers result in the church functioning like a healthy physical body with all systems working in harmony. The maturity of the leadership sets the example for members to follow. Out of that example, the body of Christ in that local church will mature to serve in many ways. Giftedness is not limited to rigid categories. As needs arise, mature believers growing up under spiritual leadership will respond to needs in natural ways.

I have been thrilled to see mature believers step up to the challenge ready to meet the needs that are obvious to them. A person who sees a specific need is the likely person who has the gift and ability to meet that need. Mindful awareness can be one way that the Spirit of God awakens the gift in a person. The passion that motivates a person to serve without need for recognition is amazing to witness. A young professional woman saw families at church exhausted from caring for children with multiple disabilities. She posed a respite care program where volunteers took care of the children while the parents took time to get needed rest, to strengthen relationships, to attend small groups for spiritual growth, or to even have a date night. This program lasted for a number of years until the children became adults and the families developed coping skills to balance familial, social, emotional, and spiritual needs.

A man in corporate sales had a natural gift of evangelism. He became distressed when he saw a single young man trying to support a woman struggling in a troubled marriage. The evangelist said he did not know anything about discipling, but he felt compelled to mentor the young believer. He sat in his car in front of the young man's house and prayed for the Spirit's wisdom. He talked with the man and expressed his concern that supporting the married woman was not wise and he should put her in contact with a woman from church to help her. While well meaning, the man showed confusion about what was wrong with his behavior. Sharing a common passion for hunting, the evangelist invited the friend to go hunting with him the next weekend. Startled by that request the man's reply was, "But next weekend is not hunting season, that's against the law." The evangelist look at his friend and said, "Exactly, and what you are doing with the woman is against God's Law." The message was understood and the evangelist realized he could disciple believers to a closer walk with God.

Another couple had experienced God's enrichment of their relationship. Seeing other couples struggling, they wanted to share how the Spirit of God transformed their relationship. They met with church leaders and presented the ideas for a marriage mentor program. A team was put together of mature couples who were willing to come alongside of people who were struggling. Out of that ministry came a number of couples renewing their vows. Still others told of how the mentoring couple showed by example how to have a Godly marriage. That couple's passion and example accomplished what marital therapy had not for many couples. This was a graphic witness to the Holy Spirit at work through believers willing to serve from their Core being.

My wonderful wife, Terry, is a person who in her Core being is naturally welcoming to people to make them feel included and comfortable. When she meets a person, she quickly comes to know the important things—are they married, how many children do they have, what are the kids names and ages, where are they from, what do they do, and so on. Amazingly, not once does the person feel like she has been interrogating them. The next time Terry sees the person, she will welcome them by name, inquire about the children, and learn more about them.

Terry's Core being expresses through the gifts God gave her. When she expresses those gifts at church, people feel included. During the week, she invites people to church who are new to the community or who appear lonely or isolated. Her gifts of hospitality and mercy are how she serves. When we operate from our Core identity, being who God intended, the expression of service is natural. Such service is an offering to the Creator that is a sweet aroma that ascends to heaven and to the nostrils of our Creator.

Chapter 4

SERVING GOD WITH OUR WHOLE HEART

Doing the Master's Will

A servant who is loved and valued by his master naturally wants to serve eagerly, willingly, and obediently. Any request made by such a master becomes the directive of the day. Since the Creator is just such a master, simply put, you and I strive to do His every request from our Core existence. Peter expresses our sentiments in this way, "You love him even though you have never seen him. Though you do not see him now, you trust him; and you rejoice with a glorious, inexpressible joy." (1 Peter 1:8 NLT) That love is the motivation by which we serve our Creator and the inexpressible joy is the product of awe that He, a non-material being, loved us so much that He took material form.

Contemplating all that Christ has done for us on the Cross of Calvary, is doing through us today by His indwelling Spirit, and is preparing for us at the right hand of the Father, how can any believer not want to serve in a manner that brings glory to Him. Living from our Core being makes it easy to know and to do the Master's will. When He left this world, He did not abandon us. He left us in the care of the Holy Spirit who reveals to us how we are to serve with the unique gifts He gave each of us. But how do we know His will?

In addition, when we learn His will, what resources do we have to accomplish the task?

There are scores of self-help materials on different aspects of the Christian life. They rightly challenge believers to live a Godly life. However, believers find themselves taking these materials and treating them as a recipe to produce the right behavior. This emphasis focuses on socializing Christians to live from the Relational self rather than expressing from the cleansed heart and the renewed mind. Living from our Core being means expressing service in a way consistent with how our Creator intended.

✍ *Journal time—Knowing God's Will Is a Process*

Using your journal, contemplate the following verses from a Core perspective. Remember that the Creator made it possible for you to know Him through your Core being.

1. Reconciliation through the death of Christ was the first step by which humanity can know God's will.

> "For <u>God's will</u> was for us to be made holy by the sacrifice of the body of Jesus Christ, once for all time." (Hebrews 10:10 NLT)

How does reconciliation make it possible for Core identity to become executive over the Relational identity and our old sin nature?

2. Transformation is the next step in the process, made possible by reconciliation. It empowers our Core being, making us able to honor our Creator.

> "Don't copy the behavior and customs of this world, but let God transform you into a new person by changing the way you think. Then you will learn to know <u>God's will</u> for you, which is good and pleasing and perfect." (Romans 12:2 NLT)

What actions characterize the Relational self?
What transforms our identity?

How does Core identity think differently from the Relational?
How does transformed thinking relate to knowing God's will?

How is God's will good, pleasing, and perfect? Hint: substitute these words—holy, honoring, and whole or complete.

3. Core transformation is directed from within by His Spirit, who indwells, seals, convicts, and comforts the believer's Core being.

"And the Holy Spirit helps us in our weakness. For example, we don't know what God wants us to pray for. But the Holy Spirit prays for us with groanings that cannot be expressed in words. And the Father who knows all hearts knows what the Spirit is saying, for the Spirit pleads for us believers in harmony with God's own will." (Romans 8:27 NLT)

How does the Holy Spirit mediate differently than Jesus Christ with God, the Father? Hint: explore the words—justification and sanctification.

If we were reconciled to God by the work of Jesus Christ, what does it mean that the Spirit pleads for us "in harmony with God's own will?"

4. Core identity follows God's will by choosing sexual purity over lustful passion.

"For God's will was for us to be made holy by the sacrifice of the body of Jesus Christ, once for all time." (Hebrews 10:10 NLT)

"God's will is for you to be holy, so stay away from all sexual sin. Then each of you will control his own body and live in holiness and honor—not in lustful passion like the pagans who do not know God and his ways… God has called us to live holy lives, not impure lives." (1 Thessalonians 4:3-8 NLT)

"Run from sexual sin! No other sin so clearly affects the body as this one does. For sexual immorality is a sin against your own body. Don't you realize that your body is the temple of the Holy Spirit, who lives in you and was given to you by God? You do not belong to yourself, for God bought you with a high price. So you must honor God with your body." (1 Corinthians 6:18-20 NLT)

How are holiness and sexual sin counter to each other?

How do Relational identity and Core identity look at the physical body differently?

What beliefs set the boundaries for Core identity to avoid sexual immorality?

What overriding Core intent prevents immoral behavior?

What Core emotions replace the lustful passion of the Relational identity?

5. Core identity shows further depth of character by submission to earthly authority as God's sovereign agency. This ultimately demonstrates our submission to the Creator whom we serve.

"For the Lord's sake, submit to all human authority—whether the king as head of state, or the officials he has appointed. For the king has sent them to punish those who do wrong and to honor those who do right. It is <u>God's will</u> that your honorable lives should silence those ignorant people who make foolish accusations against you." (1 Peter 2:13-15 NLT)

Consider Jesus' answer in Mark 12:17 regarding Roman authority when asked by the Pharisees about paying taxes to Caesar. Jesus respected Roman authority as ordained by God the Father. The Pharisees attempted to trap Him so He could be accused of insurrection and wrong doing before Roman authority. Even when brought before Pilate, Jesus was seen as innocent by Roman authority. However, to fulfill God's promise, Jewish authority committed perjury so God's redemptive purpose would be accomplished.

How does humility and respect before governing authority relate to living from our Core identity?

If you wish, you can explore the ideas around unjust governmental authority as found in dictatorships. But do not lose sight of God's ultimate sovereignty over all of creation and all authority on Earth. Please limit this area so you are not distracted from the big picture of living in accord with God's will.

Do we, from a Core perspective, have the right to tell God-ordained authority that we believe they are wrong?

How does submitting to God-ordained authority demonstrate Core faith in the Creator's sovereignty?

Other than the exception where a governing authority prohibits one's open declaration of faith in Christ, how does submission to authority silence ignorance?

How did Stephen act in submission to authority, though he was stoned to death for blasphemy?

Remembering that submission to authority is an act of obedience to God's will, how does one practically demonstrate that in twenty-first century life?

Evidence that God Honors Submission to Earthly Authority

We, as elders of a local church, were faced with the problem of improving the antiquated air-conditioning system for our church building. Upon receiving bids from three contractors, the costs were too high for the congregation's means. We began praying for wisdom on how to meet a definite need with the aging equipment in the building. The elderly members were finding it difficult to attend services in the summer time for health reasons.

A suggestion was made that we ask for a bid from an HVAC contractor from a sister church in the north-central part of the state. He presented us with bids that were within our ability to pay. But then he informed me that on checking into his contractor license fees in our county, it would add three thousand dollars to the bid and we were back where we started with the high cost. He then posed that he could come on a Friday afternoon and between then and Saturday evening he could have the furnaces installed and running for Sunday's services. Church members liked the idea because it would save money and we could afford the project.

I found myself becoming convicted in relation to the 1 Peter 2 passage of submitting to governmental authority thereby honoring God. I prayed about the problem and the seeming unfairness that a contractor received no reciprocity between counties. Finally we let it go on the basis that honoring God in our decisions both individually as well as corporately as a church was the testimony we wanted to reflect in our community presence. We would accept that we were to submit to the local zoning and construction codes as the representatives of God's ordained leadership albeit secular. Four months had passed in the throes of this dilemma and the heat of the summer was becoming oppressive.

The hand of God was so obvious in what happened next that it was nothing short of divine intervention, a truly amazing experience of awe. In the next set of bids we put out to different local HVAC contractors, two bids were even more expensive than before. A third bid came in lower than all the bids, even lower by another thousand dollars than the out-of-area heating contractor's bid. In checking out the bid with this independent installer, he assured us it was correct. He called our attention to a part of his proposal we had missed. His plan was to use existing ductwork and other delivery methods that were tried and true and much less expensive.

This was a true modern-day lesson in the faithfulness of God. Between 1 Peter 2:13-15 and Hebrews 10:36, I had powerful evidence that God keeps His Word and honors faithfulness. Yes, even for what some may consider a luxury. By yielding to the city zoning and building codes, God had made it possible for us to be faithful stewards of His money. Submission to local authority, using patient endurance as we remained faithful to God's explicit will, the great reward came in God's demonstration of faithfulness to me personally as well as to the local church who enjoyed the comfort of the heating and air conditioning system for the years that followed. What an incredible God is our God!

6. The process of knowing <u>God's will</u> results in an attitude that manifests in Core identity because of spiritual maturity. Joy, intimacy, and gratitude reflect a depth of character that can only come from a servant who desires to fully do his master's will.

"Always be joyful. Never stop praying. Be thankful in all circumstances, for this is God's will for you who belong to Christ Jesus." (1 Thessalonians 5:16-18 NLT)

How can one be joyful "always?"
How can one pray "never stopping?"
How can one be grateful "for every circumstance?"
What is a servant expressing from his Core being if his attitude is seen as a consistent expression of joy, intimacy, and gratitude?

7. Evidence of maturity in the servant who is living out God's will can also be seen in how the Core identity uses the brain in an integrated manner.

"Do not stifle the Holy Spirit. Do not scoff at prophecies, but test everything that is said. Hold on to what is good. Stay away from every kind of evil." (1 Thessalonians 5:19-22)

These verses are related to the previous passage and could be considered additional features. I am including it here to illustrate how the transformed thinking of our Core identity uses the brain. Keep in mind that the Relational self is focused on the external world. The sensory information received and processed by the limbic system is done in a bottom-up manner. The emotional associations held from life experiences govern how the individual responds. The Relational self has an ongoing vigilance to protect from perceived danger. The transformed thinking of the Core self uses top-down process that is supported by true faith as expressed in Hebrews 11:1 NLT—"Faith is the confidence that what we hope for will actually happen; it gives us assurance about things we cannot see."

"Do not stifle the Holy Spirit."

Examine the phrase. Why would the Relational self not hear or listen to the Holy Spirit? How is that different from the Core self?
"Do not scoff at prophecies, but test everything that is said."

Notice that this phrase shows the difference between how the Relational and Core identity thinks. Hint: scoffing would dismiss and testing would evaluate.

Why would the Relational self scoff at prophecy? What associations might come from bottom-up process?

Why would the Core self test the prophecy? What insights would come from the top-down process of testing the prophecy?

"Hold on to what is good. Stay away from every kind of evil."

Notice this phrase also shows a difference between how the Relational and Core identity thinks. How might both the Relational self and the Core self benefit from each phrase? How might these phrases fit into the bottom-up and top-down process to arrive at knowledge of truth?

✍ *Journal Time Ends—Knowing God's Will Is a Process*

I am awestruck at how God's word was written by the Holy Spirit to communicate truth and transform human thought process to hear God's truth, to know it, and to receive it. Coming to know God's will is one example. This is clear in the Scriptures from your journal.

Decision-Making and the Will of God by Garry Friesen[10] was published in 1981. I encourage you to get both the book and the workbook because it makes clear that God's will was not a bull's eye at which to aim. So many evangelical Christians thought of the will of God as a target in the 1960s and 70s. Unless you hit the bull's eye, you were not in God's "perfect will." This was applied to one's spouse, vocation, church, location, car, house, furnishings, and so on. The place where people got off track was that they applied the verse regarding salvation to living a sanctified life of service to God. Romans 3:23 NLT says, "For everyone has sinned; we all fall short of God's glorious standard." When it comes to a relationship with a holy God, anything other than being holy as He is holy misses the bull's eye. We are unsuited for God's presence without the atonement we received through the work of Christ. Only through being cleansed by the blood of Christ may we enter the presence of a holy God.

After that, as I live a holy life, I please God. Through Christ, I am empowered to so live. To think that God's will requires making precise choices about one's spouse, vocation, or other life decisions is an example of superstitious logic or magical thinking. It is like thinking that in doing what pleases God I can still sin or make the wrong choice regarding spouse, job, and so on—that is ludicrous! I could never wrap my mind around this kind of thinking as a young adult. I had a sense that God had a plan for me that He would reveal as I walked with Him. Remember that by the Holy Spirit we learn of God's will in our daily walk. I had mentors in my life that by word and example taught me to experience the sufficiency of Christ each day.

Finding the Master's Will

Two Old Testament characters are used as examples of how some would seek God's will, Gideon and Moses. These narratives are not held up as ideals. Rather, they demonstrate the process of growth in Core faith. Believers today have an advantage over the Old Testament believer because we know of the incarnation, death, burial, and resurrection of Jesus Christ. The will of God is clearer to us because of the work of Christ and the gift of His Spirit.

The Gideon Method—Give Me Evidence that You Are with Me

Read this narrative and compare it to the Biblical passage. (Judges 6-8 NLT) Gideon, a Jew from the tribe of Manasseh, was threshing his grain inside a winepress to keep it out of sight of the Midianites lest they steal it. Israel was under oppression from her neighbors, the Midianites and the Amalekites, because she had turned from God and engaged in pagan worship. This had been ongoing for seven years. Each harvest time these neighboring countries would attack Israel and strip the countryside of all crops and take them back home with the livestock they had also claimed. This continual food theft left Israel in a state of hunger. So Gideon had crops hidden from the Midianites and was threshing them in secret.

The Angel of the Lord appeared and addressed Gideon by name, referring directly to his name's meaning, which was "mighty warrior." Gideon does not answer from his Core identity. He rejects his own Core name and complains that God has not shown His might on behalf of Israel. "Where is Jehovah? I heard the stories of His might—how He delivered Israel out of Egypt. And to what end? To turn us over to the Midianites? No, Jehovah just abandoned us to this abusive tyranny."

The Angel addressed Gideon again. "Go in the strength that you have and win the day for Israel against Midian. I am sending you." Gideon, like Moses, argues with the Angel of the Lord who knows his Core identity. "But I come from Manasseh, a weak tribe of Israel, my family's clan is the weakest and I am the weakest of my family." Gideon is not being humble. He is rationalizing to avoid the responsibility God is giving him to serve God and Israel.

The Angel reassures him that he will not be doing this alone; God will fight alongside him. Furthermore the Angel of the Lord tells Gideon that the battle he is to fight will be as easy as if he is fighting and defeating one man.

Gideon says to the Angel of God, "I want you to give me a sign as proof you are who you say you are and will carry through with what you promised. But hold on a minute. I have to get the offering for you." The Angel of the Lord promised not to leave. Gideon went home to prepare the sacrifice that may have taken him over an hour. He prepared the dough of unleavened bread and baked it. He butchered the young goat, cooked the meat (most likely by boiling it), and made a broth from the liquid in the cooking pot.

When Gideon returned, he brought with him the unleavened bread, the goat meat, and a pot of broth. Following the Angel's directions, he placed the bread and the meat on a rock and poured the broth over it all. The offering was saturated with the liquid; the bread was quite soggy. The Angel of the Lord touched the sacrifice with his staff. Fire came from the rock and consumed the soaked bread and meat. With that, the Angel of the Lord vanished.

Gideon had his sign; he became a believer that moment and reacted, "Oh no! I have seen the Angel of the Lord face to face! Woe is me, I am doomed!" However, the Lord reassured him he would not die. Gideon had become aware once again of his Core being and expressed his worship to Jehovah from his Core by building an altar that he named Jehovah-Shalom, "the Lord is my peace."

The Lord told Gideon he was to take the second bull from his father's herd. That bull was born seven years before when the Midianites became the instrument of God's judgment on Israel. With that bull, Gideon tore down the town altar to Baal and cut down the Asherah pole that was alongside the altar. Ten men were with Gideon as he carried out the instructions of the Angel of the Lord. They built a new altar that was clearly to honor Jehovah, the God of Israel. On that altar, Gideon sacrificed the bull that was used to destroy the pagan worship center of the town. It was sacrificed on a fire fueled by the wood of the Asherah pole.

The next morning, Gideon's father stopped the angry mob planning to kill Gideon for his actions. "If Baal is upset about what Gideon has done, let Baal deal with Gideon." Gideon's father reawakens himself and the crowd to the fact that Baal is merely a carved image, an inert object of worship. Jehovah alone was truly God who grieved at Israel's disobedience when they turned from Him to worship the pagan gods of Canaan. The mob became silent at the reminder of Jehovah, the God of Israel.

Gideon had received from God undeniable proof that Jehovah was with him and with Israel once again. The townspeople greeted Gideon by his new nickname, "Jerub-Baal" meaning "Hi Gideon, I see Baal hasn't gotten you yet." Every passing day that Gideon heard his nickname was a reminder to him and Israel that if Baal was really a god, he could defend himself. Each day that Gideon lived bore testimony that Baal was a false god.

So Gideon got his answer to what God's will was for him, right? Not Quite!

When the season arrived for the marauding armies of the Midianites, Amalekites, and other nations to attack and steal the harvest, Gideon came under the influence of the Holy Spirit. Gideon blew the shofar, the ram's horn, as a call to arms. All the fighting men of Israel responded to his call. Gideon was in his headquarters, the winepress, where he threshed the grain while hiding from the Midianites. Gideon asked Jehovah for a second sign that He would keep His word. "I am laying a fleece on the threshing floor. If tomorrow morning the fleece is wet with dew and the ground is dry, then I will know this is truly what you want me to do." The next morning, Gideon found the first "Sham-Wow," a highly absorbent product of recent years, when he wrung a huge bowl of water from the saturated fleece.

Remarkably, Gideon is not yet satisfied and has another request. "Lord, please don't get upset with me; but, <u>one more sign please</u>. Could you make tomorrow's results the opposite of today's? Leave the fleece dry this time and have all the ground be wet." How people came to picture God as this angry despot is beyond me. Throughout history, Jehovah has demonstrated incredible patience with all who sought Him. This instance with Gideon is a case in point; Scripture is full of other examples too. Of course, Jehovah answered Gideon's request, and now Gideon had the answer that led to action.

Gideon was the forerunner of today's postmodernist and scientist. He wanted to make sure the language was clear so he could know truth, if truth could be known. In addition, like a scientist, he was conducting research by controlling the variables so that he had accurate results. After the Angel of the Lord vanished with the first sign at the altar, Gideon only heard Him speak. How could he get visual confirmation?

The army of Israel had gathered with the encampment of marauders in the next valley. "Gideon," Jehovah said, "You have too many soldiers. Any victory will be seen by Israel as having saved themselves. Ask if any are afraid and want to go home." Gideon gave permission to 22,000 to return home, leaving 10,000 willing soldiers to form the army. "Gideon, you still have too many. Take the men to the spring-fed brook over there and tell the men to break ranks and have a drink. I want you to divide the men into two groups—the ones who drink from their cupped hands while standing and the ones who kneel down to drink." I can see Gideon trying to figure out how this test was relevant. This young man was a farmer. He did not have the military intuition to see what God would learn by this test to determine which soldiers would be right.

So Gideon did as God directed. Nine thousand seven hundred men got on their knees to drink. Gideon might have breathed a sigh of relief because that was still a significant fighting force. "Gideon," Jehovah addressed him again. "See those three hundred men who stood to drink? I will defeat the enemy with those soldiers.

Send the rest home." Gideon dismissed all the troops except the ones who drank standing. Collecting provisions and shofars from those returning home, Gideon was preparing his men and his own mind to fight.

"Gideon, go down to the Midianite camp and defeat them; but, if you are afraid to attack tonight, take your servant Purah and spy out the enemy. Listen to what they are saying to each other." You know the option Gideon took. He and Purah crawled to the camp, noticing the innumerable camels among the enemy swarms. They listened in on the conversations. He came upon one man sharing his dream from the night before. "I dreamt that a loaf of barley bread came rolling down the hill, hit a tent, flipped it, and then knocked it flat." His comrade said to him. "You know what your dream means? The God of Israel has given Gideon son of Joash, the Israelite, victory over Midian and all its allies!" The soldiers may have joked about the dream and its interpretation; but, the interpretation was spot on and was the next sign Gideon needed. The fact that they knew his name did not strike fear in Gideon at that moment.

Gideon and Purah returned to the soldiers. Gideon was energized like the men had not seen before. Gideon was suddenly Core-present, finally reflecting the meaning of his name. His Core being manifested his identity with confidence. He was truly a "mighty warrior."

"Men, get up! The Lord has given you victory over the hordes of our enemies!" Gideon broke the men into three groups with the instructions for everyone to keep their eyes on him for the signal. Divided into three groups of one hundred men each, the soldiers of Israel lined up around the periphery of the marauders' camp. Each man of God's army held a shofar in one hand and a lit torch with a clay jar shielding the light in the other hand. At Gideon's signal, they were to break the jar, blow their shofar, hold the torch high, and shout, "For the Lord and for Gideon!"

After the midnight changing of the guards, the three groups were in position at three points around the enemy camp. When Gideon blew his shofar, broke his clay jar, and held up the torch, the others followed suit. Imagine being in that enemy camp, asleep in your tent, when suddenly you are awakened by the haunting cry of the ram's horn in surround sound. The valley of the campsite echoed with the sound of three hundred shofars placed around the camp so there was no way to locate a specific source from a sure direction.

As you throw back your tent flap, suddenly you see in every direction flaming torches surrounding the camp on all sides. Three passes exited the valley. Gideon and his men had positioned themselves above the valley floor where the marauders were camped so the effects of the sights and sounds of that night provoked terror even among the most weathered soldiers. Then you hear the battle cry of Israel, "A sword for the Lord and for Gideon!" The echoes across the valley would have sounded like thousands of soldiers were attacking at that very moment. The sounds of breaking clay jars, the blaze of torch lights casting moving shadows, altering the enemy's visual acuity produced a phenomena now implemented in modern warfare—shock and awe tactics.

None of the enemy soldiers were true to their Core being in that moment. The soldier persona was in a fight or flight mode of sympathetic dominance from bottom-up processing. Hearts beating fast, minds racing in an attempt to identify the enemy, and swinging their weapons at any movement in close proximity was not how they were trained. Some followed the kings, grabbed a camel from the droves, and once mounted, spurred the camel to flee. In the chaos, the camels had more wisdom than the soldiers; they headed through the nearest pass and toward the Jordan River. Fording the Jordan, camels and riders alike put distance between them and the valley of Jezreel.

Did you notice that the battle cry was changed as if by one mind; most likely the Spirit of God? The marauding troops held the mental image that the God of Israel was standing with His sword ready to strike. Remember the dream of the one soldier? Out of their terror, each of the enemy began to swing his sword without thought or reason. The battle was death by friendly weapon. The Midianites, the Amalekites, and those from the nations of the East killed each other in the chaos of the moment. Initially they were described as hordes of locust stripping the land bare. But now they were like the hordes of locust climbing over each other to escape, dying from the sheer weight of the climbing hordes. This was Gideon's military plan, and God's Spirit was upon him. Not bad for a timid farmer!

Those who escaped the valley alive fled great distances. Gideon, to assure the totality of this victory, called on the warriors of the tribes nearby, those who had been sent home days before, to pursue and destroy the escaping enemy. Later, when asked to be Israel's king, Gideon knew God's will on that subject and rebuked the people, affirming that Jehovah alone was the rightful sovereign, the King of Israel who time and again had proven faithful in spite of Israel's turning to other gods.

I am convinced that if Gideon had trusted God earlier, the victory would have come sooner. Gideon's request for signs, first to be sure of God's identity, and then to be sure of God's direction was not the best means of faith to learn of God's will. If as a believer you have a sense of direction within your Core being that would be honoring to God, do it. Usually, like Gideon, we seek signs because the Relational aspect of self is sensitive to what others think. If our Core being is held back in our conformity to the world or even the social influence of other believers, we are unable or greatly constrained from hearing God within our heart and spirit.

✍ *Journal Time—A Process of Testing, Rather Than Trusting*
God's will for Gideon was obvious. Jehovah had chosen him to lead Israel into battle and free them from the seven years of oppression by the Midianites, the Amalakites, and the kingdoms to the East. The Angel of the Lord affirmed God's will for Gideon by three signs found in Judges 6. What were they?

1. Judges 6:12 The Lord called Gideon by his Core name
2. Judges 6:14 _____
3. Judges 6:16 _____

List all the remaining signs from the Angel of the Lord, some specifically requested by Gideon to prove that God was with him. God's patience was evident in His response to Gideon's requests. All the signs from God became the basis for Gideon to carry out God's will from Core faith.

Judges 6:18 _____
Judges 6:21 _____

Judges 6:23 _____

Judges 6:25 _____

Judges 6:26 _____

Judges 6:34-35 _____

Judges 6:36-38 _____

Judges 6:39-40 _____

Judges 7:2-3 _____

Judges 7:4-6 _____

Judges 7:7-8 _____

Judges 7:9 _____

Judges 7:10-11 _____

Judges 7:15f _____

Journal your thoughts and feelings about how Gideon's example impacts you. If you are timid or shy, how can Gideon's example encourage you to trust God to be with you?

If you sense a direction in which God is leading you, do you seek a relationship for support like Purah was to Gideon providing a reality check, mentoring, and encouraging by reminding of God's presence? Who is or could be that person of faith of the same gender who could come alongside of you. God strengthens and heals us through community.

✍ *Journal Time Ends — A Process of Testing, Rather Than Trusting*

The Moses Approach—Stand Still and Wait

Another method of knowing God's Will was one promoted by Christian leaders in the 1960s. Numerous devotionals were written about the passage we will explore in a moment. I call this "The Stand Still and Wait Method." While at Moody Bible College, I had an opportunity to go on a summer mission team to Lima, Peru, with Literature Crusades International. Classes and professors sensitized me to the fact that we needed to be doing God's will and that there was a specific way to seek God's will. So I began to ask numerous spiritual leaders that I respected how they would suggest I go about identifying God's Will regarding my summer plans—stay at home to earn money for my next semester of school or go to Lima, Peru, for a mission outreach.

104

One person suggested that I use the Gideon Method. Tell God that if it was His will for me to go He would need to provide me the money to fund the trip. Then I would know what His desire was.

That prayer never received an answer because I did not use a fleece. I did not take to that approach very wholeheartedly because I believed that was associated too closely with a mindset of Christian fatalism. "Oh, you got the money, aren't you lucky" was what I heard two Christian leaders say to another applying for the Lima team. "What does luck have to do with God's desire for my life?" I thought.

Three Christian leaders that I asked within a two-day period each referred me to Exodus 14:13.

"Don't be afraid. Just stand still and watch the Lord rescue you today." (Exodus 14:13 NLT)

The operative phrase in knowing God's will according to this passage was to stand still and wait for God to work it out. Maybe my attention deficit disorder made it hard for me to stand still and wait. But I could not accept that rationale on the premise of my sincere desire to serve God in Peru. My spirit was drawn to that opportunity as what God wanted me to do that summer. If necessary, I would somehow wait for an answer in obedience to God. As the next two days progressed, I did not find comfort in what the three leaders had told me. After lunch on the second day of my quest, I found the weekly student devotional in my mailbox. The topic of the article was "Knowing God's Will" and the author used Exodus 14:13 as his illustration. Well, now I had the answer, didn't I? A published article must make it the official answer.

I went back to my dorm room a little miffed. This passage did not make sense to me as holding the key to the knowledge of God's will for one's life. In that moment, I remembered what Dan Dunnett, the pastor of my home church, had told me about studying God's Word. "Look at the context of the verse. When was this passage written? Who wrote this passage? To whom is the passage addressed? And Lowell," he would say emphatically to me, "always look at the next verse."

There in my dorm room, I read the next verse and suddenly realized in that moment why I was confused. Exodus 14:13-14 was Moses' answer on how to know God's will or desire. Moses' answer speaks from the depths of his Core faith that God would provide an answer. The three friends had given me the right chapter, just the wrong verses. The next verses say:

"Then the Lord said to Moses, "Why are you crying out to me? Tell the people to get moving! Pick up your staff and raise your hand over the sea. Divide the water so the Israelites can walk through the middle of the sea on dry ground." (Exodus 14:15-16 NLT)

✍ *Journal Time—Frozen in Fear or Moving in Faith*
God's directive is simply that we continue on in the direction He laid on our heart, trusting Him to intervene. He will address the barriers that arise. This passage became an important principle, a means of understanding and evaluating God's direction and will in my life. The principles in this passage follow. Write how you have or could experience God's hand in the future in your life.

What direction have you sensed God leading you consistent with your passion to serve Him?

Have you continued to move in the direction that God has laid on your heart with clarity?

If you encounter a roadblock, do you wonder if God has changed His will? What can help you stay on the course when you have doubt?

Do you have a faith community encouraging you to press forward and trust that God will remove any obstacles or open new pathways? If not, who will you seek as a mentor right now?

Remember that God is responsible to bring glory to Himself through you, His workmanship. How can that truth empower you?

Your part is to remain faithful to God's will and His word from your Core identity thereby glorifying Him with every fiber of your complete being. Hold on to His faithfulness.

Moses was leading the people of God from Egypt but he also still had a bit of Egypt in him. He forgot that God had just done the impossible with Pharaoh. When it seemed Pharaoh would never allow them to leave Egypt, God intervened in a manner that Pharaoh could no longer refuse. The loss of his first born son was the most devastating blow God could bring because it undermined Pharaoh's dreams of a dynasty based on his defined future as the man-god Pharaoh who would reign in this life and continue to reign in the future through his son, his son's son, and so on.

On that basis, the waters of the Red Sea did not stop the God of Creation. He promised to deliver His people. Moses and Israel were to march ahead in faith in the anticipation that God would part the sea and allow them to cross on dry land. They could have continued to march around on land with the Pillar guarding their path. But God's ultimate plan was the annihilation of Pharaoh and his army which happened by horse, chariot, and rider being swallowed up by the Red Sea after the whole nation of Israel had crossed on dry ground. Many have debated the Red Sea crossing as myth or metaphor until only in the recent decade. Archeologists, by looking in a location never before considered, have found Egyptian chariot wheels of the era of the Exodus under the waters of the Red Sea.[11]

✍ *Journal Time Ends—Frozen in Fear or Moving in Faith*

Another Personal Vignette

The motto of my graduating class from Moody was "Faithful is He who called you." At an annual time of reflection during a New Year's Eve service, I felt I had failed in the pursuit of God's will for my life. Academics were difficult for me and I was questioning my career direction. The Lord brought that verse to mind and showed me all He had done to that point in spite of my shortcomings. I had just completed my Masters Degree in counseling psychology, was teaching in the psychology department of a community college, and was in a doctoral program in school psychology. God showed me that He was with me and that He held my future. From that night, I treasured that verse and time and again experienced God's faithfulness in fulfilling His promise to my Core being. I came to cherish the different translations of 1 Thessalonians 5:24, but the New American Standard Bible (NASB) phrasing was my favorite.

"Faithful is he that calleth you, who also will do it." (KJV)

107

"Faithful is He who calls you, and He also will bring it to pass." (NASB)

"The one who calls you is faithful, and he will do it." (NIV)

"God will make this happen, for he who calls you is faithful." (NLT)

In my reflection on the goals that I believed were God's direction for me, I came to fully realize that the life goals I pursued to honor God had actually fallen into place. I had cold, hard evidence that God made it possible for me to realize my desire to serve Him as a counselor. Often in early years, I wished that God had allowed my path in education for my profession to be more direct. In the last thirty years, I realized the diversity of my education afforded me a range of experience that helped me to minister to hurting people. I am grateful for God's faithfulness. He who drew me to Him, continues to fulfill His plan for my life.

✍ *Journal Time—How Have You Witnessed God's Faithfulness?*
Enter into your journal the Core evidence you have from life experience that points to the faithfulness of the Creator shown personally to you. How has He revealed His will for your life? Have you shared this with other believers and invited them to join you in praising Him for His intimate involvement?

✍ *Journal Time Ends—How Have You Witnessed God's Faithfulness?*

Preparing for Core Service

"Spiritual disciplines" prepare us for service.
The real intent of spiritual disciplines is not merely to develop consistent spiritual behaviors and habits, but to learn a deeper relationship with God. Discipline by itself does not assure spiritual intimacy. Saint Ignatius addressed this over three hundred years ago by encouraging a meditative process as a means of spiritual discipline that led to a deeper relationship with God. He encouraged the believer to

meditate on God's loving kindness and goodness in light of one's own sinfulness. Intimacy is the product of a thorough progressive meditation on the person of God. Through meditation on the redeeming work of Christ, we come to experience the amazing forgiveness and cleansing that allows a Holy Father God to look upon you and me, once repulsive sinners, now redeemed through His Son.

Often these spiritual disciplines are seen primarily as the result of solitude. However, growth and healing come through community. Ignatius encouraged the meditator to find a mentor to encourage genuineness, honesty, and accountability. The mentor emulates Paul as an example of faith and as a supportive spiritual father. Paul courageously said, "Dear brothers and sisters, pattern your lives after mine, and learn from those who follow our example." (Philippians 3:17 NLT) If you are a person of spiritual maturity, mentoring or discipling the young in faith is an area of service greatly needed in these times. Doing so safely and wisely means taking to heart the mindful cautions of Galatians 6:1-5 NLT.

Spiritual discipline and the resulting intimacy with our Creator can be frightening because it requires honesty on our part. Our Relational identity perceives inadequacy and hides in shame like Adam and Eve, even with the knowledge that the Creator knows us intimately. When we approach God from our Core being, we come with gratitude that He embraced us with loving kindness and forgiveness. Our Core being approaches His throne boldly because we have experienced His grace.

Dallas Willard, a professor of philosophy at the University of Southern California, was passionate about people having a deep experience with God. You will find a wealth of information on spiritual formation and discipleship at www.dwillard.org, a website dedicated to educating believers about discipleship.

✍ *Journal Time — Preparing Our Core to Serve*

What practices do you mindfully use to draw closer in your relationship to Jesus Christ?

How often each day do you find a spiritual song, a Bible verse, a sermon message, or a devotional reading coming to mind?

Mindfully observing, what is the stimulus that makes those thoughts conscious?

How does your day change after those spiritual encounters?
What could you do to increase such encounters in your daily life?

✍ *Journal Time Ends—Preparing Our Core to Serve*

"Spiritual gifts" are the means of service.

Identifying the gifts of each believer is another area that has been the focus of faith communities. The principle of Scripture is that when each member of the local church is actively exercising their gift, there is unity, growth, and health in the church. Teaching on spiritual gifts that seeks to identify the gift of each church member does so on the premise that these be defined, assigned, and expressed for the growth of the church.

I find believers genuinely trying to figure out what their spiritual gift is so they can do what might honor and please God. Questionnaires, curricula, and study materials were developed to assist people in the identification of their gifts. The intent is laudable, but the process emphasizes the doing of your gift from the Relational self rather than the expressing of your gift from your Core being. These gifts or abilities are the Creator-endowed talents He gave each person in his or her Core identity at birth as a means to express what ultimately praises the Creator.

Paul used the analogy of the human body as a metaphor of the Church. Every part of the human body participates for a purpose. If one part should become ill or weak, the whole body can suffer. A cold is a simple example. A cold can block the nasal passages so less oxygen gets to the lungs. With the supply of oxygen restricted, the red blood cells do not deliver an adequate supply to the brain and muscle cells. The result is a feeling of tiredness and lack of energy. All this is the result of congested nasal passages. At that moment the nose is the weakest member of the body and proves Paul's observation that one small area of the body affects the health of the whole. This principle can be illustrated with a broken bone, a strained muscle, or a headache to show how the state of health of one part affects the whole body.

A faith community needs every member to be actively expressing his or her gift to be spiritually healthy. One weak member of the faith community can drain the expressive resources needed to bear testimony to the message of salvation as the power of God.

Every person who is a member of the body of Christ in a local church contributes to body health by expressing his gift. If some part of our body is ill, we do what is necessary to nurse it back to health. Our Core being wants to participate in a healthy church body, so we can express our gift for the purpose of unity and health. It seems logical that we would want every member to live from his or her Core being so we as the church will be healthy, thrive, and glorify our Creator God.

What an amazing God, that when He created you and me, He knew He would delight in how we would serve Him and one another from our Core identity. A wellspring of unique talents exists within the faith community because of the Creator's design. God's will, that we live holy lives, makes us qualified to serve. God's gifts bestowed on each one's Core being at conception are intended to honor Him and to serve one another as co-members of the body of Christ. These gifts are present in the non-believer because of the Creator's design and are unique Core abilities that in their use by humanity are proof of the Creator's existence. Ultimately, He has given us gifts to use in expressed service and how we choose to express those abilities to honor our Creator comes from within.

Core desire to serve the Creator comes from Core consciousness. Humanity has six areas of consciousness that reflect the image of God. We explored these ideas in the prior two volumes. Like God, we are conscious of our actions, our emotions, our sensations, our knowledge, our volition, and our energy. Service is expressed by conscious use of all of these features of awareness. Volition and energy or intent are the most relevant in serving God and each other. These are the most related to internal, top-down processing of information by the Core self's use of the brain. Choices consciously made from one's Core being are the least directed by what others think we should do. Core self seeks the "could," rather than the "should," as the personal basis for service.

As mentioned earlier, the list of gifts show the wide variety available to serve the body of Christ. But labels do not identify these gifts in the daily activity in the body of Christ. What makes a faith community viable is that those who are capable step up and become involved when, where, and however the need presents. A person living in his or her Core being is naturally attracted to certain areas of service that are consistent with their gifts. The involvement comes from the energy of intention. Finding an opportunity to serve others based on giftedness brings depth to Core faith.

To make this clearer, I take you back to your identity assessment. Look at your adjectives. They reflect natural Core expressions as you defined yourself. These are closely related to your abilities. For example, if you used patient and listener as descriptive adjectives, then you might have an ability to listen to hurting people. If you used handy and patient as descriptive adjectives, then you might have the gift to make house or car repairs for someone in the faith community. Explore this concept in your journaling.

✍ *Journal Time—Identifying Your Core Gifts*

Consider the adjectives you used to describe yourself. List them again as a reminder and after each note how that adjective might be used in an expression of service.

1.
2.
3.
4.
5.

Now combine words from your list into pairs to narrow down or to be more focused on specific areas in which to serve. In what areas of service might you be able to use these natural interests and abilities?

1.
2.
3.

How have you found yourself naturally drawn to participate in these types of activities within your faith community in the past?

How does a spiritual gift expressed in service, relate to Bible reading, study, and prayer?

You may find your Core expression of service suppressed because your Relational self is judging your actions of service as inadequate. Contemplate these words.

"Pay careful attention to your own work, for then you will get the satisfaction of a job well done, and you won't need to compare yourself to anyone else." (Galatians 6:4 NLT)

This verse speaks directly to our Core intent. To become conscious of an area of needed service within the faith community is to hear the Spirit of God prompting your Core to serve. First, thank God for the prompting, pray for guidance, ask spiritual leaders for feedback, and then take action to serve. If you do not take action to serve, you will find yourself ignoring the Holy Spirit and allowing the judgment of others to silence your heart. If you believe someone else would do better than you, you are allowing your Relational self to have control. The Spirit of God spoke to you in your Core being.

By simply carrying through, by paying attention to the fact that you are serving for Christ's sake, and by finishing the task you are expressing service from Your Core being. This verse gives you the right to say, "Praise God, I did it!" These are the bragging rights that believers have in serving God.

Become mindful of opportunities to serve. Serve without judgment in the moment of carry through. Notice any doubt that comes from the Relational self and release it to the Holy Spirit. Thank God for the opportunity. Contemplate the Creator's delight in your Core being.

Write out your reflections on these ideas with the intent to become more open to the Holy Spirit's leading in serving the Creator from your Core being.

✍ *Journal Time Ends—Identifying Your Core Gifts*

I trust that you are energized by how easily opportunity for service will appear. As others witness you living and expressing service to your Creator from your Core identity, they will be challenged to follow your example. You will be the example of service that promotes spiritual health in the local church so the Creator's joy will be evident as a result.

Section 3.3: The Core Expression of Worship

"Man, so long as he remains free, has no more constant and agonizing anxiety than find as quickly as possible someone to worship." Fyodor Dostoevsky[12]

"As worship begins in holy expectancy, it ends in holy obedience. Holy obedience saves worship from becoming an opiate, an escape from the pressing needs of modern life." Richard Foster[13]

[W]orship is hard-wired within each human being. That hard-wiring leads humanity to cherish objects believed to be important to existence and identity. The above quote of Dostoevsky speaks to that human condition. Humanity can feel adrift, empty, and undefined without an object to worship. When found, humanity puts such objects of worship on a pedestal to be idealized and idolized with the hope that fulfillment follows.

The typical human response to internal unrest is to seek that which stills the unsettled heart. Unless we acknowledge that we exist as the result of a personal Creator who has a plan for us, we cannot find peace. Without that personal relationship, humanity finds nothing that satisfies. The objects of worship are expected to quiet the discontent within the human spirit but the best they can provide is a mere numbing of the heart. The result is the human being becomes addicted to worship of the material in the hope to find peace. Consider Foster's quote above.

Faith brings us to worship a Creator who we love even though we have never seen Him. We trust Him because we accept the witness of Scripture. And we experience worship as Peter describes as rejoicing with glorious, inexpressible joy. (1 Peter 1:8 NLT) May the ideas of the next chapters teach you about Core expression that relishes and cherishes the majesty of your Creator leaving you stunned by His magnificence.]

Chapter 5:

STONES OF WONDER
AND WORSHIP

Keep your journal close as you read this narrative on worship. Be mindful of the thoughts and feelings from your Core self prompted by the Holy Spirit. Record these thoughts in your journal for future contemplation.

The family was finishing the evening meal when Papa announced, "Dvir and Chava, Mama and I have some exciting news for you. This Passover, we are going to Jerusalem to celebrate this most important festival of our people at the Temple. We will worship Jehovah for freeing us from Egypt and bringing us to this land promised to Father Jacob. On our travels, we plan to do sightseeing that may not sound very exciting. We are going to visit some stones that have stories to tell us."

"Papa, how can stones tell stories? They cannot speak," said Chava.

"Chava, you know that Papa likes to tell stories that teach us about Jehovah. I am sure he will be the voice for each stone." Dvir, Chava's older brother reminded his sister how Papa taught them lessons about Jehovah. Dvir was thirteen, the age that a Jewish boy was seen as an adult and no longer the moral responsibility of the father. This meant that Dvir was considered mature enough to understand right from wrong and to choose on his own to do what was right according to Jehovah's law.

Jewish children were taught the spiritual and social aspects of life from the Torah to prepare them for adulthood. Any time questions came up about making the right choices, Papa or Mama would recite passages from the Torah that illustrated how Jehovah wanted His children to respond. As devout Jews, Elior and Dinah, Dvir and Chava's parents carried out Moses' command to teach children the Law of God at any and every opportunity in the flow of day-to-day life just like the Torah said:

> "Teach them to your children. Talk about them when you are at home and when you are on the road, when you are going to bed and when you are getting up." (Deuteronomy 11:19 NLT)

By age thirteen for boys and age twelve for girls, Jewish children knew the Law of Moses and were considered morally responsible for their choices and were therefore considered adults.

Elior and Dinah and their children, Chava and Dvir, lived in the town of Capernaum on the beautiful Sea of Galilee. Mindful of God's directive to Hebrew parents to teach their children God's law at every opportunity, Elior and Dinah had discussed with each other the plans for this special journey. Elior hoped the journey would teach the children what it meant to worship Jehovah as Creator God and as the God of Israel.

✍ Journal Time – What Spiritual Traditions Do You Have as a Family?

The Stone That Came to Life

"Children, come sit with Mama and me as we start our journey here at home and listen to the first stone tell its story."

Papa had their full attention. Papa told stories from the Torah in very exciting ways, making the story come alive. Even a story Papa told many times before sounded fresh and different; there was something new each time. This is how Papa began. "In the beginning, God created stone, water, sky, and light. These basic substances

were all that the Creator needed to make the whole universe and all
its inhabitants.

"The Creator's desire was for the work of His hands to serve
Him and to bring Him praise. Since praises are sung, each object
of creation was to become one of the many voices in the Creation
choir. Every voice was intended to blend in harmony to sing praise to
Jehovah Creator God and by their very existence bring glory to Him."

"But Papa," Chava protested, "Water, sky, stone, and light do not
make sounds by themselves. They are inert; they have no energy of
their own; they can't speak. Sounds only happen when water falls
on a rock and splashes. As the light of the Sun heats stone, the space
around the stone gets hotter. Heat makes space move about faster,
creating a wind. The wind moves over the surface of the water and
stirs the water to make waves. The waves undulate along not making
much noise until they crash on the stones at the edge of the sea. That
is what you told me."

"Chava, I am glad you listen so closely," Father would say. "Your
brother knows this as well but because he is older now, he doesn't
let his interest show. He doesn't want anyone to think he is listening
and enjoying the story too."

"And by the way Dvir, just because you are considered an adult
now, don't lose your child-like faith. Don't grow up too soon. Do you
remember what that teacher Jesus said the other day? Adults need
the simple faith of a child to enter God's kingdom."

Dvir joined the conversation. "Father—I mean Papa, you are
teaching us about the inert material of the universe that God began
with. Like Chava said, these substances had no life of their own.
They came into existence from nothing but God's command. Then
He separated them from one another to organize them for the next
step of creation."

"Very good, Dvir. You have learned your lessons well." Papa
showed his pleasure in Chava and Dvir's ability to express ideas
they had learned from Mama and him.

Papa continued with his story. "Every day God created something
new and beautiful. On the sixth day, Jehovah made all the animals
that walked on stone. Before the day was over the Creator knew it
was at that moment in His plan for His greatest work of all creation to

come into existence. He took some stone and with His hands shaped it in His likeness. Then He breathed into the stone shape He had formed and man came to life; but he was lonely. So He put the man to sleep, took a bone from the man's side, from that bone shaped a woman, breathed into her, and she too became alive. The man was no longer lonely because the Creator provided him with the perfect companion.

"When He finished creating this man and woman called Adam and Eve, He saw His image in them, just as he had planned. He declared all creation 'good;' but these human beings, made in His image, He declared, 'very good!' It pleased the Creator to walk with them at the same time every day. The voices of stone made alive delighted the Creator. Adam and Eve would excitedly share with Jehovah a new discovery they made that day about His vast creation.

"All that their eyes saw, the new sounds that they heard, the new smells, tastes, and textures that they experienced brought Jehovah to mind. They thanked Jehovah for all He made for them to share. They would sing about the day that Jehovah had given them life and one another. They joyfully treasured each moment they spent together with each other but even more so that time spent with Jehovah the Creator. These human creatures were exactly what He desired them to be. The Creator's hands gave humanity form; His breath gave humanity life; and His image gave humanity mind and voice. He Jehovah God had transformed inert stone into living humanity from whom He desired the expression of worship and praise.

"Chava and Dvir? Mother and I often looked at you as you have grown up and marveled at the Creator's handiwork that each of you represent. Jehovah has truly blessed us. We see each of you as His gift to us. You remind us by your very existence of how wonderful are the works of His hands. We cannot praise Him enough. You represent the story of the first inert stone we planned to visit via this story. That inert stone of today's story was shaped into a man and woman and given life. That was how humanity was created and cherished above all of creation by the Creator."

"Please, Papa; tell me another story."

"Chava, it is time for bed; good night. Now go to bed. Tomorrow will be a busy day."

The next morning dawned clear with a warm breeze gently removing the chill of the night. "Dvir and Chava?" Papa called for the children to rise and come to breakfast. "Today and tomorrow we will pack to begin our journey to where we will visit the third stone."

Dvir appeared to look disinterested, but his next comment betrayed his real thoughts. "Papa – you already told us about only one stone – the use of stone to create Adam and Eve. They were the first inert stone of worship that Jehovah made alive and made them to reflect His image. When Jehovah breathed life into them, they came alive and spoke. No longer inert, they praised God for His creation with their God-given voices. We have still have not seen the second stone. Are we going to do that before we begin our journey in the next two days?"

✍ *Journal Time—How Does This Story Bring You to Worship?*

Papa responded to Dvir's insight, "Very good Dvir. Now that I have the whole family's attention, I planned to visit the second stone this morning from right here. The second stone is too far north for us to make that journey at this time. I will begin that story as we finish breakfast.

The Stone That Saw a Rainbow

"Adam and Eve had it so good in the Garden of Eden including so much good fruit on the trees. Jehovah had only one requirement of them. He told them to enjoy the fruit of all the trees of the Garden except one. They were not to eat of the Wisdom Tree because the fruit from that tree would make them know about good and evil. But the serpent deceived them; they ate the fruit, learned about good and bad, and hid from Jehovah because one bit of knowledge they learned was that they were naked. Their shame gave them away, and God punished them by putting them out of the garden and protected them by keeping them away from the tree of life. Jehovah did not want them to eat, to know, and to live in that state forever. He covered their nakedness and sent them into the world so they could start a family.

"Even though they had been created in His image and were holy and innocent, they lost their innocence when they sinned and disobeyed God. Outside the Garden, they had two sons and one killed the other because of jealousy. Later they had another son named Seth who learned of Jehovah and followed Him. But each generation of humanity continued to sin bigger and bigger. Each generation became more violent and forgot their Creator. However one man, Enoch, was so righteous that Jehovah miraculously took Him out of this world. God removed Enoch when he was 365 years old so that he did not have to see continual wickedness.

The day came where Jehovah regretted ever creating humanity. He contemplated wiping out all humanity and starting over.

"Papa."

"Yes, Dvir?"

"That is horrible. Where is the awe in that part of the story?"

"Good question, Dvir. Awe and horror are actually closely related. In awe, we don't want the moment to stop. We feel amazed by the beauty that we see. In horror, we want the moment to stop and wish that we had never witnessed what was seen. To witness something that is very disgusting, maybe even ugly and evil, is hard for our mind to understand. We become horrified. Repulsed with horror, we want it to stop, but we can't ignore what we see because it is so unusual that we want to understand what it means. This is the introduction to our next stone."

"In the days of Noah, humanity did whatever they wanted to do if it made them feel good. Right and wrong was not important, feeling good was. People did not think about what Creator God desired. In fact, no one thought about the Creator at all; well, almost no one. Noah was a righteous man and lived the way Jehovah God desired. He lived for five hundred years before he had children, three sons – Shem, Ham, and Japheth.

"What praise Jehovah had for Noah. The remainder of humanity deserved to be destroyed for the selfish, violent, and evil behavior that they displayed rather than reflect the Creator's image.

"Jehovah spoke, 'Noah, I want you to build a boat.'

"'Okay, God. But what's a boat?' said Noah.

Dvir groaned, Chava giggled, and Mama rolled her eyes. Papa continued with the story. "As Noah listened, Jehovah gave Noah very exact instructions how to build this boat. When Noah heard the size of the boat, he thought to himself, 'maybe some of the people will change their minds when I tell them judgment is coming. That must be why God wanted extra space.'

"Then God told Noah he was to get two of every kind of animal, one male and one female, so when the boat was finished the pairs of animals could come on board and survive the deluge. Of the clean animals, Noah was to get seven pair.

"Noah warned people that God planned to destroy the Earth. Noah also preached by his lifestyle that judgment was coming. Each time Noah picked up an inert tool and put it to use, that tool resounded with the message that judgment was coming. With every question anyone asked, Noah answered expressing God's displeasure with humanity's wickedness; and then Noah told them if anyone chose to believe, the Ark was available to them as a tangible means of God's salvation from coming judgment.

"A total of eight people accepted Creator God's means for salvation. Noah, his wife, his sons, and their wives boarded the Ark when directed by God. All the animals were already onboard in their respective compartments. Then God lifted the gangplank and closed the door. The Ark was sealed shut by Jehovah, so it would be waterproof.

"A whole week went by with no sign of rain. When the door first closed, some people might have been concerned. However, as each day passed without rain, Noah's neighbors became more convinced that Noah really was crazy. But, the rain did come. When the rain began, the profusion of water was amazing. Water poured down from the sky. Water burst out from the stones. The pounding on the sides of the Ark accompanied with screams of terror and pleas requesting entry did not last long. A few short hours after the deluge began the sounds of distress from humans and animals ceased.

"But the deluge continued without letting up for forty days. When not one more drop of water could be found to add from either above or below, the rain stopped. The only sounds now were the wind and waves outside the Ark. Inside the Ark were the sounds of the last eight human beings on the Earth conversing and the animals gently lowing to one another.

"A full year went by from the first drop of rain until Noah, his family, and the animals could leave the Ark. There were signs of hope in the passage of time onboard. First was that the Ark floated without signs of leakage from poor construction or signs of breaking apart from the violence of the deluge.

"Signs of hope continued. On the fortieth day, the rain stopped. The waters began to recede until five months after the first drop. Noah and his family heard a 'thunk' sound as the Ark rested solidly on the stone of Mount Ararat. Noah and his family looked out the window at the top of the Ark seeing only water in every direction. Two and one half months after the Ark stopped moving; mountain peaks poked out above the surface of the water.

"Noah waited forty more days and released a raven. The raven did not return to the Ark. Ravens had such strong wings that they could fly to the distant mountain peaks and rest there. Noah also released a dove that returned by the end of the day. One week later, Noah released the dove again. That evening the dove returned with an olive branch in its beak. Noah knew that plant life was growing. When the dove was released one week later, it flew off and did not return.

"How amazing that while Jehovah was cleansing water, sky, and stone of evil humanity, He still personally watched over every life in the Ark. The Ark, inert wood, under the influence of sky and water drifted until the water subsided according to Creator God's plan. The Ark of salvation came to rest on an inert stone, Mount Ararat. That mountain of stone stands today, many years after Noah and the Flood, as an inert witness of God's faithfulness. He keeps His promises to humanity.

"Dvir and Chava, do you think that the stone's voice has made its story known?" asked Mama.

"Actually, the stone of Mount Ararat had more to say," said Papa. "Listen to this last part of the story. When the gangplank was lowered, the wild animals were herded out of the Ark. Then Noah and his family disembarked. I think even though the Ark was sitting still for a couple of months while the ground dried out, Noah and his family shared an awe experience as they finally stood on solid ground. Noah did not just fall to his knees and kiss the ground out of gratitude to see dry land again.

"Noah found a huge stone and rolled it to where it seemed right for an altar to be built. He had each family member find as large a stone as they could handle and pile it with his to finish building the altar. Each one contributed to the building of the altar as the place of communal worship. Noah sent his sons to get the animals set aside as a sacrifice to Jehovah. Noah's next actions were to place wood on the altar, to slay the animals that God desired as a sacrifice, to sprinkle the altar with their blood, to lay the animals on the altar, and to light the fire.

"All eight souls, the only living human beings left on Earth, stood watching the smoke ascending to Jehovah God as Noah thanked Jehovah for the salvation He had provided. That moment of worshipful reflection increased in awe as each memory and thought of all God had done came to mind. The awareness was vast. Jehovah's salvation had preserved each one of them.

"Noah did not know how long they stood there worshiping Jehovah in that moment of awe, with their words of praise as the sacrifice burned. The fire was dying down, the sacrifice consumed. Before any of Noah's family moved from where they stood by the altar, the Sun shone brightly and the sky burst into splashes of color. Never before in human history had such an event occurred. A mouth-dropping awe was the result of the bursts of color that God named for them – 'a rainbow.'

"Chava, when you see a rainbow, what do you do? You usually run to Mama or me and want us to see it too, don't you? And we all, even Dvir, go 'ooh' and 'aah' in awe at the display of colors. Imagine seeing the very first rainbow like Noah and his family. There on Mount Ararat, the droplets of water still suspended in the atmosphere from the Earth drying out, caught the sunlight. An arc of color spread from one side of the horizon up, across, and down touching the other side of the horizon. A palette of color was distributed across the sky in the shape of a bow. It was as if an artist's brush holding all the colors in sequence had made a bold, sweeping stroke on the canvas of the sky.

"God spoke then, 'Noah, whenever humanity sees the rainbow, it will be a reminder of my promise that I will never again destroy the earth by means of a flood. Humanity will see the rainbow and remember My promise; and that I, Jehovah, Creator God keep my promises.'"

As Papa reflected on the story, he voiced his personal thoughts. "The stone of Mount Ararat witnessed Jehovah's righteous anger and protective love. This most graphic demonstration of judgment by the deluge to cleanse stone of wicked humanity and by the Ark to provide salvation for the righteous illustrated that message so clearly. Even more so, the awe stirred by Jehovah's reminder to His promise displayed by each rainbow across the sky—He will never again destroy the Earth with a flood."

✍ *Journal Time —How Does this Story Bring You to Worship?*

After a few moments of thoughtful sharing by Chava, Dvir, Mama, and Papa about the stone of Ararat, Papa gave out the chores of the day.

"Chava and Dvir, you can help today by completing your assignment. Tomorrow morning we will start our trip to visit the third stone. Okay everyone, enjoy your day, and do your part to prepare for the journey."

The Stone That Was a Pillow

Early the next day the family began their journey. Balaam their donkey was packed with all they needed for the trip. Even Balaam seemed eager for the travel ahead. The family was healthy and accustomed to traveling on foot as was normal in those times. Since they generally traveled 20 to 25 miles in a day, Papa thought they would make it to their next stone in five days. The weather remained nice as they traveled south following the route closest to the Jordan River. The family arrived a day early at the town called Bethel. It was here that Papa's third stone was located.

"Dvir, do you know the meaning of the name 'Bethel?' " was Papa's first question.

"House of God," answered Dvir without a moment's hesitation. Dvir rightly felt proud of himself for knowing the answer.

"Excellent, Dvir." Papa was proud of his son who loved to learn. With what Dvir knew, he could usually figure out answers that led to other ideas and insights.

"Everyone, notice that field over there on the side of the road. Tomorrow we will return and we will listen to the story of a stone in that field." With that comment, Papa led them to the inn in the village of Bethel where they would spend the night.

After a good night's rest, the family gathered for a breakfast of bread, cheese, and milk in the field Papa showed them along the road. The hillside stretched quite a distance along the road that passed through the valley. Between the road and the base of the hill, flat stones were strewn about. "Papa," said Chava, "It looks like someone cut steps in the hillside and pushed the hewn stones down into the valley."

"Chava, that is an interesting thing to notice. I want everyone to look around and find a stone that is just the right thickness to hold up your head as you lay on your side. When you find one that fits, bring it here where we have eaten breakfast." Papa sent them off with their assignment. He had already seen one that worked for him. He retrieved it and brought it back. Mama returned with hers. Chava chose one that she could manage. But everyone started laughing when they saw Dvir lugging a long one. His face showed strain and determination as he arrived. He let his stone fall with a heavy thud.

Papa began the story of the stone of Bethel.

"Isaac and Rebekah had twin boys; Esau was born first and then Jacob. At birth, Jacob's hand was gripping his brother's heel as Esau was born red and hairy. Jacob followed quickly behind. Esau grew up favored by his father and became a hunter and farmer. Jacob was favored by his mother and became a shepherd. One day, Esau came home very hungry to find Jacob had fixed lentil stew and bread for their father. 'Jacob, please give me something to eat. I am starving.'

"Jacob saw this was the perfect opportunity to win first place. 'I am happy to give you a bowl of stew and bread, for a price. Give me your birthright.'

"In his state of hunger, Esau did not think twice about what he was doing; he agreed to Jacob's terms. Jacob accomplished the first part of his goal to have the rights of the firstborn. Rebekah knew what Jacob had done but kept it to herself.

"Years later, Isaac was a blind elderly man and sensed he was near death. He called for Esau and told him that he was going to bless him as his heir. However, first Isaac requested that Esau hunt in the open

127

country for the wild game to prepare his favorite savory meal. After the meal, Isaac promised to bestow the blessing on Esau.

"Rebekah, the mother of the twins, overheard Esau and Isaac's discussion. She sought out Jacob and hurriedly made preparations to disguise Jacob to trick her blind, infirmed husband to bless Jacob in place of Esau. After all, it was rightfully Jacob's blessing because Esau had been so careless about his birthright selling it for a bowl of stew. Rebekah knew how to fix the meal so that young goat's meat tasted like the game Isaac requested. Jacob reminded his mother that he did not have the body hair of Esau. Rebekah already had that problem thought through as well. She sewed sheepskin around Jacob's arms and neck so he would feel like Esau if Isaac touched his son; she then gave Jacob a suit of Esau's clothing that still held the odor of the hunt.

"Jacob brought in the meal he had prepared and served his father. Isaac tasted the food and it tasted just as he remembered. Still, Isaac was suspicious. 'Son, come closer.' Isaac felt Jacob's arms made hairy by the sheepskin covering. He smelled the odor of the huntsman on his clothes. Except for Jacob's voice, everything else indicated it was Esau. With that, Isaac gave Jacob the blessing that established Jacob as legal heir.

"Only minutes went by after Jacob left the presence of his father when Esau appeared. 'Father, I have your meal. Eat and enjoy it. When you have finished, I will be ready for your blessing.' Isaac began to weep as he recognized he had been deceived. Esau did not understand his father's tears until Isaac could compose himself enough to tell Esau that he had already given the blessing to Jacob. At Esau's pleading for some kind of blessing, Isaac offered the dregs to Esau.

"You will live away from the richness of the earth, and away from the dew of the heaven above. You will live by your sword, and you will serve your brother. But when you decide to break free, you will shake his yoke from your neck." (Genesis 27:39-40 NLT)

"Not a very cheerful or promising blessing. It left Esau plotting that as soon as his father died, he would kill Jacob. When Rebekah overheard Esau's plans, she encouraged Isaac to send Jacob to her brother's to find a proper wife that was not a Canaanite. Esau had married two Canaanite women to the disappointment of his parents. Isaac and Rebekah did not want Jacob to have a wife who worshipped any god but Jehovah.

"Isaac called Jacob to his bedside and told him to go to the town of Haran in Paddan-aram to his brother-in-law Jacob's Uncle Laban. There he was to look for a wife. You understand Jacob was going to his mother's country to escape his brother's murderous anger and to find a wife that would worship Jehovah.

"Jacob left early in the morning. He walked fast knowing that at anytime his brother might pursue him to murder him. At the end of the day, tired from the consistent pace to put as many miles as possible between himself and Esau, Jacob finally made camp. Jacob looked for a stone that was as comfortable as possible to use for a pillow. That very first night after he left home, Jacob was in this very place where we are today. As he lay down, he fell quickly to sleep. As soon as he fell asleep, Jacob had a remarkable dream.

"The dream was that of a stairway between heaven and earth on which angels were ascending and descending. God stood at the head of the stairs and introduced Himself to Jacob in his dream.

'Jacob, I am the God of your grandfather Abraham and the God of your father Isaac. The ground upon which your body is laying is yours. I am giving it to you and your descendants. Your descendants will be many and will fill this land in all directions—North, East, South, and West. You will have kings and rulers among your offspring. Through your children will all humanity receive blessing.'

'Be assured that my presence is with you wherever you go. I will protect you in this your land and even when you are away from here. There will come a day when I will bring you back to this, your land. I have promised you these things and will not leave you until I provide every promise I have made to you.'

"On waking from that dream, Jacob instantly knew the presence of God was in the place where he was camped. He was struck that there was nothing remarkable about the countryside to be aware of its significance. No Canaanite religion marked this place as a mystical portal. They assigned other locations with those traits where their pagan gods went between the physical and the spiritual worlds.

"This land was rich and fertile, prime land to hold. God declared this beautiful land as his by virtue of the promise God had made to his grandfather Abraham and his father Isaac. He told Jacob that now He Jehovah had claimed it for Jacob and his offspring. This land of promise was the best in all of creation.

"Jacob realized in that moment that this was a holy place. He had met Creator God who knew him by name and spoke personally to him. Jacob was stirred by fear and awe when the Creator gave him the promise that He Jehovah God would personally care for him while he was away and when he returned to this land. What a 'send off' for Jacob! He was leaving family behind so that his life might be spared. This place was where he personally met Jehovah. Such a nondescript place, yet God had given Jacob and his offspring deed to this land. As his awe subsided, Jacob fell back to sleep.

"Upon arising the next morning, Jacob took the stone which was his pillow and stood it upright to mark this holy place. He anointed the stone with oil, and he named the place 'Bethel' – the House of God because this was where he met God.'

"Here in this place, Jacob made his personal commitment to God. 'Lord, if you remain with me, protect me, and provide food and clothing through my journey, and return me safely to my father's home, then you will be my God. This stone will become my place to worship you. I will present to you one tenth of all that You give me as my act of worship.'

"Papa, that is such a beautiful story."

"Chava, I am only one half done with this story. May I continue?"

"Jacob continued on his way to his planned destination, his Uncle Laban's, to find a wife according to the wishes of his father and mother, Isaac and Rebekah. Jacob traveled on eagerly over the days that followed. He was energized by the promise that the God of his grandfather and his father was with him.

"Jehovah proved to be with Jacob. The first people he met were shepherds at a well in Haran who knew his Uncle Laban. He met Rachel just moments later, herding Uncle Laban's sheep to be watered at the well. Welcomed to his uncle's house, Jacob offered to work for his uncle without money for seven years so he could earn the right to marry Rachel. His uncle tricked Jacob into marrying Leah, Rachel's older twin. Jacob worked seven more years to finally marry Rachel. Then Jacob worked seven more years to earn herds of sheep and goats as his very own. No treachery of Laban and his sons worked because Jehovah kept Jacob safe.

"In the twentieth year, God told Jacob it was time to return to Bethel. Both women agreed that their father had no plans to grant them an inheritance. Both realized their father Laban saw them as possessions and not as his daughters. Leah and Rachel knew that Jacob was quite different in that even though he did not love them the same, he did value them as God would have him.

"Jacob took Leah, Rachel, and all his children, his servants, all his sheep and goats, and all else of value and began his journey back to Bethel. When Laban heard of Jacob's departure, he and his sons pursued him. The night before Laban caught up with Jacob, God appeared to Laban during the night and warned Laban clearly that he was not to harm Jacob in any way.

"When Laban caught up with Jacob, he continued his deceptions hoping to trap Jacob in lies. Finally, Laban confessed to God's warning. Jacob stood up to Laban and told the truth of all Laban's deceptions and broken agreements. Jacob piled stones for an altar with only his wives and children helping. Laban sat with his entourage eating and drinking at Jacob's expense. Jacob sacrificed to God and told Laban this altar was a boundary. Laban, true to form, had to make it as if it was his idea so that he could appear in control. Laban named the place "Witness pile," claimed to be the builder of the monument, and spoke the vow…

"May the Lord keep watch between us to make sure that we keep this covenant when we are out of each other's sight. If you mistreat my daughters or if you marry other wives, God will see it even if no one else does. He is a witness to this covenant between us.

"I will never pass this pile of stones to harm you, and you must never pass these stones or this monument to harm me. I call on the God of our ancestors—the God of your grandfather Abraham and the God of my grandfather Nahor—to serve as a judge between us."

"Jacob had no qualms with that agreement. He had twenty years of proof of God's favor and protection. Not even the blustery words of Laban provoked any fear in Jacob. Laban kissed his daughters and grandchildren "Good-bye" in the morning and returned home.

"Jacob told his family and everyone else with him that they were to destroy all their pagan idols, purify themselves, and to dress in clean clothes because they were going to Bethel to honor Jehovah. When they arrived at Bethel, Jacob's family saw this very field filled with these flat pillow stones that we see here today. Only one was standing upright. Rachel often heard Jacob tell of this marker of Jehovah's promise and excitedly pointed to the only upright stone in the field. Jacob found his pillow stone still standing after twenty years marking Bethel, the place Jehovah made His promise to Jacob. Jacob looked at the stone marking where he slept and dreamt. His heart was in his throat. That stone withstood the elements for twenty years. What Jacob heard the stone say was, "I remember the dream and the promise. I stand witness that Jehovah God kept His word and brought you home.' Jacob did not kiss the stone and thank it for standing there in the field all that time. No, Jacob rearranged the stones of the original altar and offered a sacrifice to worship God who had fulfilled every word He had promised twenty years earlier. God's response to Jacob's worship on the stones of Bethel was to give Jacob a new name, 'Israel,' meaning 'May God Prevail.'

"The old name spoke to Jacob's old nature of deception, the supplanter. He replaced Esau as heir to their father Isaac. The name

'Israel' described his persistence when contending with God. The name Israel stood for the nation reflecting God's persistence to be acknowledged while they contended with Him. Israel, formerly Jacob, had seen that his God Jehovah was with him, protected him, and brought him back to his land.

"The pillow stone became the pillar stone, the marker of where God would return Israel. The stone altar at Bethel was the place that many of Israel's offspring would worship Jehovah. God had introduced himself to Jacob, now called Israel, as El-Shaddai, God Almighty. The place known as Bethel, the House of God, represented to Israel as a nation an altar of praise where God eventually made a nation of slaves into landholders as He, the God of Israel, the man once called Jacob, had promised.

"Dvir and Chava, our Jehovah is an amazing God. By the way children, if you look to where the sun rises in the morning that is east of here. About one day's journey from here to the other side of the Jordan River is where Laban caught up with Jacob. That is where "Witness Pile" is, the boundary that Laban agreed before the God of Jacob he would not cross to harm Jacob. We did not go there to visit that stone because that is not our land. It is exciting to have been here in Bethel where Israel once worshiped on an altar here. That altar does not exist anymore since we have the Temple in Jerusalem where sacrifices are made to atone for sin in the earthly presence of God.

✍ *Journal Time –How Does This Story Bring You to Worship?*

"Children, we are going back to our night's lodging to pack. We will travel a little further to our next lodging at Bethphage where we will see one more stone before going to Jerusalem and to the Temple.

The Stone That Became the Altar

The City of Jerusalem laid spread out before the family as they looked at Jerusalem from the Mount of Olives. Arriving at Bethphage from Bethel after Papa's story there, the family got a good night's rest. The family walked to this place called the Mount of Olives this morning.

"Children, you will never guess why this place is called the Mount of Olives." Papa loved to tease them but not in a mean way. That was how Papa made them think more deeply about things. Dvir came right back at Papa with, "I know, this is really made up of piles of olive pits that were thrown away here over all the centuries. The many piles of olive pits became this big mountain range. Eventually some of the pits sprouted and grew so now there are many olive orchards."

Papa chuckled at Dvir. Then he encouraged the family to sit in the shade in the olive grove along the road. Mama opened the food basket and provided bread and cheese for lunch. Papa cleared his throat and pointed to a hill they all could see. "There is our next stone that has its witness story. That is Mount Moriah."

"Out of a pagan culture, in the city of Haran, the country of Paddan-aram, the region of Mesopotamia, which was the center of the world in its day, came a man named Abram, who worshipped Creator God. His neighbors worshipped the Sun, the Moon, and sculpted images of their many gods and goddesses. But Abram acknowledged only the Creator. The Creator had shown that He rewarded those of humanity who believed in Him.

"Abram was tending his sheep when Jehovah spoke to Him. 'Abram, I want you to leave your home here and go to a place I will show you. That place will be the land of your children who will be innumerable.' Well, Abram went home and told his wife Sarai about his conversation with God. 'What, you want me to move? I finally got everything organized. I am comfortable here.' said Sarai.

"'Yes. I must obey my God. He blesses me for honoring Him,' was Abram's answer. So, in spite of her protest, Sarai packed up to follow Abram, as was the custom of those times.

"When Abram arrived in that land of promise with his wife Sarai and his nephew Lot, God continued to bless Abram for his expressed faith in God, but Abram did not have the promised heir. After God changed their names to Abraham and Sarah, the couple in their old age finally had a child, Isaac. By then Abraham was a very wealthy and widely respected man in the land of Canaan.

"When Isaac came of age at 12 similar to our Dvir, God told Abraham to go to a mountain that God would show him, a place that Abraham did not know, where he was to sacrifice Isaac, his only son. He packed his donkey with a brazier of fire and a fresh hewn bundle of wood. He, Isaac, and two young men began the journey. The young men were a distraction and companionship for Isaac. Abraham, a man of faith, was so absorbed in his thoughts, ruminating on why God was making this request of him, that he should sacrifice this son, his promised heir.

"As Abraham saw God's intended destination, he told the young men to stay with the donkey. Abraham gave Isaac the wood to carry while he took a knife and the brazier of fire. Together they continued on foot up the mountain. Abraham had taught Isaac to worship God as one who kept His promises. Without the distraction of the fellowship of the two young men, Isaac noted the obvious. 'Father, we have the wood and the fire, but where is the animal for the sacrifice?'

"The struggle within Abraham not to stir undue anxiety in his son nor to show his grief to his son was great. Abraham stated from faith, 'Son, God will provide a lamb for the sacrifice.' Arriving at the sacrifice site, Abraham arranged some stones to form an altar, arranged the wood on the altar, had his son lay on the altar, and then he tied his son. Isaac showed faith in his father and in God by complying with what was happening.

"Abraham raised his arm, knife in hand, to plunge the knife to end his son's life in obedience to God. It was God's voice that stopped that moment of sacrifice, 'Abraham, do not harm the boy. I know you truly fear me. You have not withheld anything from me, not even your only son.'

"Abraham lowered his arm with gratitude and relief. Abraham cut his son's bindings and embraced Isaac. In that mindful moment, Abraham spotted a ram that must have strayed from its herd and became entangled in the underbrush. Released from his entanglement, the hobbled ram was put on the altar in Isaac's place. Isaac stood with his father at the altar, a worshiper, not a sacrifice. Both father and son began weeping, worshiping, and praising Jehovah. How sweet the praise in that moment, both father and son in joint worship to Jehovah God! The sweet odor of the burnt offering ascended to Jehovah as an atonement for their sin.

"Abraham named that place of worship, both the stones of the altar and the stone of the mountain itself as witnesses, 'Jehovah-Jireh,' meaning, "the Lord will provide." What a demonstration of faith by a father to his son that Jehovah, the God of Israel, intervenes and meets the needs of the faithful. No, the story is not finished. Those stones witnessed more. This mountain witnessed the truth of that name to all of Israel at another time.

"A long time after Abraham, Israel had received God's promise of its own land. At that time, David was King of Israel. What seemed innocent enough on the surface, King David called for Joab, the Head of the Armies of Israel, to appear before his throne. The King instructed Joab that he was to take a census of all Israel from the town of Dan in the North to Beersheba in the South. Joab knew it was not right to do and objected. But you can't refuse the King.

"What was wrong with knowing how many people were in Israel? Would a king not benefit from knowing his people and also how many soldiers were available? Nine, almost ten months later, Joab gave the statistics to King David. Because of David's heart, David felt guilty, and confessed his wrong to God. David admitted to Jehovah that victory for Israel came because Jehovah fought on their side. Numbers were not Israel's strength; Jehovah was their strength. David thought of Him by the name Moses used as Jehovah-Nissi, the Lord is our Banner.

"Jehovah taught Israel in unique ways so that they might learn of who Jehovah really was. Jehovah gave David three choices—three years of famine, three months of running from enemies, or three days of severe plague. Well, that seemed like a no-brainer. David chose three days of plague. The illness raged through the land until God stopped it outside Jerusalem on Mount Moriah. Some seventy thousand had died in those three days.

"A man named Araunah who was a Jebusite owned the top of Mount Moriah at that time. He conducted his business there where he threshed grain. It was at the threshold of his business that Jehovah stopped the Angel who was spreading the plague just as he was preparing to enter Jerusalem. The plague displayed Jehovah's justice and the end of the plague displayed Jehovah's mercy. When David asked Jehovah to lay the blame on him, he was told to go to Araunah's threshing floor and offer a burnt offering.

"David approached Araunah and told him of his desire to buy his place of business to build an altar to sacrifice unto Jehovah. Araunah was willing to donate it so the king could fulfill his sacrifice. However,

David knew that he must purchase the place of business if the sacrifice was truly from him to Jehovah. After the king bought that place, the altar was constructed; the building was torn down to provide the wood for the fire; and the oxen that had ground the grain were the animals for the burnt offering to Jehovah. Jehovah received His rightful due in that sacrifice and was pleased by the sweet aroma.

"Chava and Dvir, do you know why this is so significant? Nine hundred years before, on the same site David built his altar to Jehovah, Abraham built an altar to sacrifice his son. A few years later Solomon, David's son built a Temple there where God could live amongst His people, Israel. The priests who had conducted worship in the Tabernacle of the Wilderness officiated in Solomon's Temple to worship God with burnt offerings as Jehovah instructed through Moses."

Papa pointed so the family would look. "The temple you see over there is not Solomon's. It is the temple built by Herod in the last sixty years to replace Solomon's Temple that was destroyed by Nebuchadnezzar. The priests do the same acts of worship in that temple today exactly as Jehovah commanded through Moses in the Torah. And here we are nine hundred years after King David and there stands that same witness stone. For almost two thousand years that stone, Mount Moriah, has witnessed the truth of its name, Jehovah-Jireh. Do you remember what that means?"

"Yes Papa. It means the Lord will provide. This is the most wonderful stone of all," said Chava. Dvir grunted in agreement. He was eager to worship at the Temple as an adult for the first time and to witness how different it was from the synagogue back home in Capernaum.

The family left the Mount of Olives and returned to Bethpage where Papa had found lodging for the week ahead. Mama prepared the food for the Sabbath meals with Chava's help. Papa and Dvir unpacked the load Balaam carried, put him in his stall, and fed and watered him. Even donkeys were to enjoy Sabbath rest. The family settled in on time to welcome the Sabbath.

Papa prayed, "Jehovah, on this special Sabbath we celebrate your gift of rest. You created for six days and then set the seventh day aside as Sabbath. We remember that we are the work of your hands. We thank you for making us in such a wonderful way. We also remember that You loved us, Your children, so much that you rescued us from slavery in Egypt. You were patient with us and forgiving even though we complained. You faithfully led us to the land you promised to Father Abraham. You fought for us, protected us, and defeated our enemies. You provided for our needs.

"Jehovah, we Israel Your chosen people shamefully turned from You to worship pagan idols. These figures were made by the hand of human beings out of inert substance that only exists because You spoke it into existence. How foolish humanity is to believe that what we created with our hands has power greater than You.

"Jehovah, I am grateful that inert stones exist as memorial markers that remind us that You keep your promises. These inert reminders left by the Patriarchs remind us of Your promises, of Your presence, of Your abundant mercy, and amazing love. All of these stones exist in a Sabbath state. That which is inert is inactive, naturally at rest, and by that state gives the Creator, Sabbath praise. Amen."

Papa gave the Sabbath blessing. The family sang together songs of praise to Jehovah. Papa joined Mama reminding Dvir and Chava how Jehovah allowed Israel to come under the rule and oppression of strange kings over the centuries. That was the wake up call to Israel that Jehovah was the only true God. Papa reminded Dvir and Chava that the Roman soldiers they had seen during their travels think of themselves as conquerors who rule Israel. In truth, God's people were still ruled by Jehovah. He alone was their sovereign.

✍ *Journal Time –How Does This Story Bring You to Worship?*

"To think, Jehovah still loves us in spite of how we have treated Him." Those were Papa's last words before the nighttime prayer; then the family was tucked in bed for a night's rest.

The Stone That Could Not Stand Still

Sleep was blissful for all but Dvir. That morning, Dvir awoke energized for the important day ahead. He excitedly hurried his family so he could get to the Temple to worship as an adult. The turtle doves were cooing their morning song. All through the journey Mama reminded Chava not to play with the doves. Mama did not want Chava to become attached to them because they were the sacrifice for each member of the family when they went to the Temple.

They stayed in Bethphage, which was only a Sabbath day's walk to Jerusalem. That referred to the distance that the scribes had determined from the Torah was an acceptable distance to walk on the Sabbath without breaking God's Law. Carrying the cage with the doves, Dvir led the family from Bethphage along the Mount of Olives to the Eastern Gate of Jerusalem and through the Shushan Gate of the Temple. Stairs at each gate took the family higher up into the Temple.

The first open area surrounding the Temple was called the Court of the Gentiles where people from many foreign countries gathered. Clothing, customs, and language differed among these tourists. Latticed screens surrounded the Temple courts with openings where warning signs were posted that said that any Gentile or unclean Jew who went beyond that point would be put to death.

Dvir became intimidated by the sheer size of the area. Papa who had worshipped in the Temple a number of times, quietly took the lead. Papa led them to the east gate called Beautiful where fourteen steps took them higher. Mama explained to Chava that this area was the Court of the Women and it was the farthest into the Temple that females could go. Mama and Chava followed Papa and Dvir only as far as the fifteen steps of Nicanor's Gate.

Through that gate was the Court of Israel where laymen worshipped and that was the farthest that Dvir and Papa could go. That court went around the Court of the Priests that contained the furnishings of worship used by the priests to fulfill their spiritual service to Jehovah in the Temple. Chava and Mama watched as Dvir and Papa approached a priest, giving him the eight turtledoves, two for each family member. One was for a sin offering and the other for a burnt offering.

Music was playing there in the Court of the Priests and was joined by voices from the surrounding Court areas. The words and melody reflected the spirit of praise to Jehovah for delivering Israel from slavery, for cleansing their sin by accepting the shed blood of each sacrificial animal, and for receiving their praise from the aroma of the burnt offering.

The family returned to Bethphage at noon to continue their celebration of Sabbath rest for the remaining three hours. Papa prayed thanking Jehovah for accepting their worship as Sabbath ended.

On Sunday morning the family travelled from Bethphage to Jerusalem. Papa noticed unusual activity taking place at the entrance of the Eastern gate. People were throwing their cloaks and robes to cover the street. Others were taking palm fronds and spreading them on the road. The family stood curious about what might be happening. Chava asked another little girl her age about what she knew about the excitement. "Jesus is coming," she said. "Who is Jesus?" asked Chava.

A man approached the Eastern Gate of Jerusalem on the road from Bethphage just one hour after the family arrived. The road was lined with crowds of people who spilled into the city street as well. The excitement of the people was contagious. The man's facial features were not very handsome and his nature was not one of natural charisma. He was astride a young donkey that seemed pleased to carry his master. When the family seemed so puzzled by what they observed, the crowd began cheering and shouting...

"Praise God for the Son of David!"

"Blessings on the one who comes in the name of the Lord!"

"Praise God in the highest heaven!"

"Papa, Chava and I saw those men early this morning leading two donkeys in Bethphage. Someone called the man sitting on the young donkey, Jesus from Nazareth." Dvir was noticing and commenting on the different activities. "Papa, who are those men in those long robes who look so important? Oh! Of course, those are Pharisees. The look on each of their faces is quite sour. The one who is close to the man riding on the donkey is scolding him. He wants the man to tell the crowds to be quiet and go home. I've got to get closer." Dvir returned almost as quickly as he left. "Papa, I know that you are not to talk back to the Pharisees because of their authority. But that man Jesus just told the leader, 'if you tell the people to become quiet, the paving stones on the street will cry out and speak in place of the crowd.' Papa, he said something that fits your stories. 'The stones will bear witness to who he is.' That Pharisee turned so many colors of angry red. I also heard the leader tell the other Pharisees to wait for another time without so many witnesses."

When the family finally pushed through the crowds to arrive at the Temple, Jesus was there. Animals were running loose in the Court of the Gentiles. There were upturned tables and money from all over the world was spilled on the ground. Many of the coins were still rolling in different directions. Jesus spoke with a serious voice filled with great authority. He told the people that they had no right to treat God's House, a place of prayer, like a marketplace and a place for thieves and robbers. Again, Pharisees were looking on with veins bulging in their necks because they were so angry.

The days before Passover were different because of all the attention to this man Jesus. The family took in a few more sights and returned to Bethphage for some quieter days. Pharisees were making more of a presence in public as if watching and listening for something specific to happen. On Wednesday, Dvir went with father to the Temple carrying two more turtledoves for another sacrifice. Much was on Dvir's mind about Papa's stories of the stones of witness and the answer Jesus gave to the Pharisee, "if the crowd stopped praising God, the stones of the roadbed would be given a voice to cry out in place of the crowds."

The next few days went by so quickly. On Friday morning, the family was caught in a crowd when they walked from Bethphage to the north side of the Temple to explore other parts of Jerusalem. The family saw many angry people at the Antonia Fortress that housed the Roman garrison responsible for keeping order in Jerusalem.

Pontius Pilate was in Jerusalem to assure that peace was maintained during the celebration of the Passover. Caiaphas, the High Priest of Israel, turned Jesus over to Pilate saying that Jesus called Himself "The King of the Jews" thus an enemy of the Roman Empire. Caiaphas expected Pilate to find Him guilty and put Him to death. When Pilate held court as Roman governor of Judea, he determined that Jesus was not guilty. Papa, Mama, Dvir, and Chava arrived as Pilate was attempting to quiet the crowd and release an innocent man.

The face of this Friday crowd was glowering and hateful. These same people were in the Sunday crowd just days before, smiling as they welcomed Jesus as the Messiah saying, "Praise God for the Son of David." Now this crowd was saying, "Crucify Him! We will not have this man to reign over us!"

Papa took his family back to Bethphage. Everyone was quiet, even a little scared. Papa began to pray to Jehovah. "Adonai, Lord God of Israel, my heart is heavy. I have been waiting for Messiah to come. I have heard people mention this Jesus these past three years. Was He Your Anointed One?"

"I remember hearing Him saying at one time that His Father loved the world so much that He gave His only Son to die for the world so that whoever believes might have everlasting life. If you gave Jesus your son on this day as your sacrifice, I believe in Jesus, Messiah, who came to suffer that we can be made right with You. I left Jerusalem and the Stone of Mount Moriah because I did not want the children to witness how awful a crucifixion is. The narratives of all the stones of witness that I have shared with the children were Your messengers to bring us back to you. Here on Mount Moriah You did not withhold your hand but required of yourself what you did not expect from Abraham. You stopped the plague of sin and death on this mountain that by His stripes we might be healed.

"I suspect this Jesus Your Beloved Son is dying at Golgotha, on Mount Moriah, a third sacrifice on that altar stone. Today my family was a witness of what You are requiring of Yourself and Your Son that You did not require of Abraham. You, Oh God of Israel; in this hour of darkness that just fell; You have left Your Son to die alone. All for our sin, my sin, and Dinah just said for her sin also. Thank you for what you are doing. I know there is more to this story that you will reveal in time. Maybe our family can be a witness that is not inert. We want to share with others that the Messiah suffered and died for our sin so they can know and worship Jehovah and thank Him for His love.

Papa took his family to the Temple to worship that Sabbath morning and to offer up the remaining turtledoves for the family's atonement. The priests and Levites were dutifully carrying out the sacrifices for the day. No one mentioned anything about the previous day's events. The number of worshipers was less than usual. The Temple atmosphere seemed very heavy, more somber than expected.

The family returned to Bethphage and waited for the evening hour when Sabbath was over to pack their things for the return home.

Elior, Dinah, Dvir, and Chava left Bethphage to go home that Sunday morning. Their hearts were sad and each step they took felt so heavy. Balaam their donkey seemed of a different mood though. His demeanor was one of light footedness and hope. By Tuesday, they were half way home. The events of the week were still fresh in their minds. Physical distance from Jerusalem was no help. By Tuesday afternoon, there were other travelers catching up with them coming from Jerusalem. Energy and happiness seemed to spur them on.

"Why are you so upset and sad?" one man asked Elior; to which he responded, "Did you not hear about what happened to that man called Jesus? Last Sunday, the people were welcoming Him as Messiah singing 'Praise God for the Son of David!' as He rode into Jerusalem. On Friday, the people rejected Him at the Roman Court of Pilate screaming as if He was the worst of criminals, "Crucify Him!""

"Elior, did you not hear about what happened after Friday afternoon? Two of Jesus' disciples took Him down from the cross and buried him in a tomb on Friday evening before Sabbath began. Caiaphas the high priest approached Pontius Pilate and told him that Jesus' followers planned to steal His body. As a safeguard, a number of strong Roman soldiers rolled a stone in place over the grave. Caesar's seal was affixed to the stone to assure that it remained closed. Roman soldiers were left to guard the burial site from Friday evening on.

"On Sunday morning, a huge earthquake knocked out the Roman guards. Caesar's seal on the stone was broken. The huge stone over the opening of the tomb was found rolled away from the opening, and the tomb was empty. Different followers reported seeing Him throughout the day on Sunday. He showed them the scars in His hands and feet. Some touched Him to make sure He was real. Still others ate with Him. He is alive! What exciting times in which we live!" Elior was weeping with his family over this wonderful news; the sadness was gone. In its place were tears of joy. The Messiah came, lived among humanity, died, and rose again to fulfill the promises Jehovah had made with humanity many generations past. The huge stone that was intended to hold Him in the grave, sealed shut by Caesar's command, and guarded by Roman soldiers to assure the Jewish rulers that He would remain entombed, had no power to accomplish what human authority expected.

Chava and Dvir thought about what the stone from the tomb might say to the foolish men who thought they could keep the Messiah in the grave. The picture that came to mind was that stone expressing rumbling laughter at the foolishness of those men of power who believed they could keep the incarnate Creator confined by death. "He is not here. He is raised," is what the stone would say. He who spoke stone into existence; who gave humanity breath; He kept His promises to Adam, Noah, Abraham, Isaac, Jacob, Moses, Joshua, David, and many others. By His death, He kept His word to free humanity from sin. By His resurrection, He made reconciliation possible for anyone who might desire to have a restored relationship with Holy God.

✍ *Journal Time –How Does This Story Bring You to Worship?*

Do stones speak? Ask Dvir, Chava, Elior, and Dinah. They invite you to join them in awe and worship of the Creator Jehovah God.

Chapter 6

THE SECOND CORE EXPRESSION—WORSHIP

What Is Worship?

My dear friend Wil shared with me from his biblical education and seminary training the origin of the word worship. The derivation of the word came from old Anglo-Saxon words: "weorth" or worth meaning value and "scipe" or ship indicating shape or quality. As Wil shared how the word "weorthscipe" became worth-ship and then worship, his face glowed with the beauty and depth of his personal experience identified with the development of the word worship in the English language.

Worth-ship is our expression of worth to our Creator. To the frustration of those who like concrete answers with organized steps, worth-ship can take many forms in many different settings in a multitude of ways. The Creator does not tell us how to worship because the ability was part of His creatorial plan and is available within the mind of all humanity. His desire is that our worship keeps Him as the focus. You and I are to express His worth to Him, praising Him for who He is, and thanking Him for all He has done to make it possible that sinful humanity can enter His holy presence. Have you known Christians who struggle to express what Creator God means to them? Might they struggle because they have not yet arrived in their walk with God where they are free from worry and judgment? Picture Paul's act of worth-ship as he spoke publicly in the manner that he wrote to the Roman Christians.

> "For I am not ashamed of this Good News about Christ. It is the power of God at work, saving everyone who believes—the Jew first and also the Gentile. This Good News tells us how God makes us right in his sight. This is accomplished from start to finish by faith. As the Scriptures say, 'It is through faith that a righteous person has life.'" (Romans 1:16-17 NLT)

Paul takes worship further in Romans 12 as he encourages believers to worship God with their material, physical being.

> "And so, dear brothers and sisters, I plead with you to give your bodies to God because of all he has done for you. Let them be a living and holy sacrifice—the kind he will find acceptable. This is truly the way to worship him." (Romans 12:1 NLT)

Paul points out that our choice to keep our physical bodies from sensuality and impure behavior is worth-ship. We worship when we express praise to our Creator with our senses and actions, avoid actions that are associated with immoral behavior, and dedicate mind and body to express the value we have for Him. His words to the church of Corinth express this clearly:

> "Don't you realize that your body is the temple of the Holy Spirit, who lives in you and was given to you by God? You do not belong to yourself, for God bought you with a high price. So you must honor God with your body." (1 Corinthians 6:19-20 NLT)

I trust that from your Core being you are expressing the value you place on all the Creator has done for you. Your actions expressed through your physical being whether in public or private, whether at church or at work, whether seen or unseen, at any moment of your day speaks worth-ship from your Core being to your Creator.

The Hermeneutics of Worship

"Yours, O Lord, is the greatness, the power, the glory, the victory, and the majesty. Everything in the heavens and on earth is yours, O Lord, and this is your kingdom. We adore you as the one who is over all things. Wealth and honor come from you alone, for you rule over everything. Power and might are in your hand, and at your discretion people are made great and given strength. Our God, we thank you and praise your glorious name! ...

Then David said to the whole assembly, 'Give praise to the Lord your God!' And the entire assembly praised the Lord, the God of their ancestors, and they bowed low and knelt before the Lord and the king." (1 Chronicles 29:11-20 NLT)

"I heard the voices of thousands and millions of angels around the throne and of the living beings and the elders. And they sang in a mighty chorus: 'Worthy is the Lamb who was slaughtered—to receive power and riches and wisdom and strength and honor and glory and blessing.'

"And then I heard every creature in heaven and on earth and under the earth and in the sea. They sang: 'Blessing and honor and glory and power belong to the one sitting on the throne and to the Lamb forever and ever.'

And the four living beings said, 'Amen!' And the twenty-four elders fell down and worshiped the Lamb." (Revelation 5:11-14 NLT)

The passages quoted above are depictions of two different times and locations where worship is expressed. In the first, King David is leading the nation of Israel in worship that anticipates the fulfillment of David's dream. David wanted God to have a permanent dwelling place with the Children of Israel. Though David was disqualified as the builder, God chose Solomon David's son to complete the task. The worship lead by David on this day was the kick off of the Capital Campaign that would fund the Temple. Upon completion of the Temple, the Tabernacle that was never intended to be a permanent dwelling as they traveled to the Promised Land could finally be dismantled. This day was a day of rejoicing because it stood as evidence of the faithfulness of Jehovah on Israel's behalf.

The second passage is of a worship service yet to be held in a future Promised Land. Prior to His death, Jesus told His disciples He was leaving them to prepare a dwelling place for them where He lived. When it was complete, He would bring them to the place He prepared with them in mind. This place will far outshine Solomon's Temple because the glory of that Temple will be from the Lamb of God who was slain for us. No one will destroy that Temple. No sin will exist in that place because the Lamb of God had been victorious over sin and death.

The common theme in both events is the worshipers falling down in the presence of Jehovah God. My Core excitement anticipates being there with you, mouth agape at a worship service that could not be accomplished before then. Thousands and millions of angelic voices, harmonizing with the four living beings, the twenty-four elders, and every creature in Heaven, on Earth, under the Earth, and in the sea. For the first time since Adam's sin, all creation will bow in worship before the Creator with pure hearts, minds, and bodies. Now that is the worship service I eagerly anticipate sharing with you.

Hermenutics is the art and science of interpretation of Scripture.[14] This area of study examines the meanings of words in the original languages of both the Old and New Testament. Hebrew and Greek words used for "worship" have a richness in the original languages that the English translation lacks. The term "worship service" is often used in protestant churches and Jewish synagogues to identitfy the primary gathering of congregants. The activities that take place in that service follow a proscribed order that may include an invocation, prayer, congregational singing, announcements, an offering, Scripture reading, a sermon, a closing song, and a benediction. Congregants may sing standing, eyes closed, hands raised, or body swaying to the music. The actions used in corporate worship may be the means to a deeper connection with God. However, an outsider may see patterned, predictable, and dispassionate behaviors by the congregation and be unsure of how those behaviors make one closer to God.

True individual or corporate worship is far from dispassionate. The evidence lies in the meaning of the Biblical words translated as worship. These words describe the actions used by the worshiper to express to God's worth. The words that described the behavior in the Temple, the synagogue, or in the early church would transform personal and corporate worship. As we explore these words, allow your mind to picture the original intent in a very concrete way.

The first Hebrew word is Shachah, which means to do reverence, to bow down, to crouch down, or to lay prostrate. When we come into the presence of the Creator, we have entered the throne room of our Sovereign Lord. This act of worship acknowledges that He is greater than we are. Jesus rises from His throne on the right side of His Father and comes to us with extended arms. We are welcomed into His presence. He reminds us we are joint heirs with Him because of His shed blood. Because of His work, He tells us we can enter the throne room boldly, find mercy, and receive needed help. Social convention makes it unlikely we would enter church and find people laying physically prostrate in worship. But what is to prevent that attitude from being present in your conscious mind when you walk into the church auditorium?

✍ *Journal Time–Compare Psalm 95:6-7 and Hebrews 4:14-16*

Halal has the meaning to praise, to rave, or to boast about God as an expression of your adoration. Have you ever bragged about God? When a loved one dear to us achieves something outstanding, we are quick to rave about his or her accomplishment. One theme of worship in Israel was the nation boasting about how God delivered them from Egypt. Paul used a parallel Greek word to encourage the believer to boast in the amazing way that God accomplished His plan of salvation.

✍ *Journal Time–Compare Psalm 34:1-3 and 1 Corinthians 1:28-31*

Tehillah is a word that signifies bursting into spontaneous song. The cover of this book was chosen because it illustrates this expression of Core worship. Micah and Papa were enjoying time together at the park on this day. All the play equipment in the park quickly lost its novelty on his third descent down the spiral slide. Micah's foot slipped on an acorn shaken from the live oaks by a windstorm a few days before. The half-grown green seeds captured his attention. The acorns were sparsely scattered about. As Micah found them, he gathered them one by one. When his hands became full, he found a flat spot on which to pile his collection. He worked hard for ten minutes to gather as many as he could find.

Suddenly, Micah scooped up the collection in both hands, carried them about with his arms extended, and unexpectedly burst into song. His words did not have to rhyme. The melodic tones in his voice filled the empty park. He was so enraptured in that moment of praise that he was unaware of my presence. That image of my grandson bursting into spontaneous praise in his moment of awe at God's creation is what Tehillah means. Can you envision becoming so caught up in God's Word and the theme expressed by those passages, that you suddenly burst into song? In a church service? Unaware of the presence of others? Socialization can quickly suppress such worship as the Relational self is afraid of embarrassment, paying attention to the environment rather than the internal Core connection to the Creator.

✍ *Journal Time–Compare Psalm 40:1-3 and Acts 16:22-30*

Guwl is another beautiful act of worship not likely to be expressed in a corporate worship setting, unless it is scheduled as part of the service. The word describes a person who is caught up in a state of intense emotion that results in carefree jumping, dancing, and clapping for joy. As you compare the following passages, keep in mind that David is the likely author of the psalm and the word translated as "rejoice" is the Hebrew word Guwl. The passage in 2 Samuel 6 shows David worshiping God in this manner and encountering contempt for the abandon characterized by his worship behavior. Think about Michal who shows contempt for David's worship behavior. What is the social rationale that Michal uses? How did David handle the matter from his Core being?

150

✍ Journal Time–Examine Psalm 118:24 and 2 Samuel 6:12-23

If you would like to study a list of fifty-eight Hebrew words that are worship related, consider the following resource. (Hebrew Praise Words—www.justworship.com/hebrewpraisewords.php)

Four Greek words are used for worship. Like Hebrew counterparts, these words describe physical actions that express the condition of the worshiper's heart. Proskuneo is the expression of a lover showing the depths of her love for her beloved with a kiss. To bow down, to show obeisance, or to kneel before are other actions related to this word. Our worship of our Creator is to be displayed in a manner that others have no doubt about our reverence and adoration of Him. As Jesus ascended to Heaven, He blessed the disciples and their worship was displayed by physical reverence.

✍ Journal Time–Examine Luke 24:50-53 where proskeuno is used.

Latreuo is the expression of worship that reflects the state of our heart in every aspect of life. To be in love with someone means the desire to cherish that person can be seen in everyday life. Love provokes us to find any and every opportunity to serve our beloved. Our Core being invests energy and thought to find ways to please our beloved. Think of how that looks when applied to worship of our Creator after all He has done for us.

✍ Journal Time–Examine Hebrews 12:28 where latreuo is used.

Eusebo is worship that shows reverence to God as one would show a parent. A worshiper is devout or one who holds another in awe. Think of how our Eternal Father promises to provide for all our needs through Jesus His Son. An ideal father is sovereign, provides for his child's needs, keeps his promises, and shows his child how to live a balanced life. Our Eternal Father God shows all those qualities to His children. The natural response to such a provider would be to hold them in awe.

✍ Journal Time–Examine Mark 6:6-7 where eusebo is used.

Doxa is the last word meaning dignity, glory, honor, and praise. You may realize it is reflected in an English word we use to title a chorus often associated to worship, the "Doxology." It reflects a verbal and vocal expression of praise to God. Most believers are acquainted with the words—"Praise God, from Whom all blessings flow."[15]

✍ *Journal Time–Examine Ephesians 3:14-21 where doxa is used.*

Such rich imagery comes from the original languages of Scripture. Whenever you hear someone say the word "worship," may these various images spring to mind, especially one suited to describe the state of your heart as you show your adoration to the Creator for His great love.

The Roots of Worship

Humanity is hard-wired to worship as is evident in the Creator's design in Adam and Eve. They sought Him out and walked with Him in the cool of the day. Adam and Eve as innocent sinless humanity witnessed untainted creation before the fall. Both expressed praise to the Creator as only innocence can. However, you and I have a greater appreciation of the Creator's love than Adam and Eve could ever envision. We stand awestruck at the fact that Holy God sent His uniquely begotten Son to draw us to Himself even though we hated Him. Adam and Eve witnessed their son Abel worshiping the Creator from his Core being. Cain out of jealousy from within his Relational self resented his brother.

God saw Abel's sacrifice as a genuine expression of worship and found it pleasing. Cain showed the effect of his parents' sin and God's curse on humanity when his worship was unacceptable. Both had opportunity to worship God as He desired. Cain's naive answer was to end his shame by ending his brother's life. He had opportunity to give what God desired but refused. The very first generation of humanity after the Garden of Eden showed the ability to worship. But Cain's worship reflected praise of himself for his labor. He did not acknowledge the Creator's existence nor did Cain give credit to the Creator for what He provided. While humanity is hard-wired to worship, humanity can only express genuine worship of the Creator when He is acknowledged.

Infancy and Worship — The early developmental signs of worship are seen in the child's natural attention to its mother as nurturer.

Satisfying the child's needs brings the preverbal child to gurgle, babble, smile, and coo. The infant shows pleasure and gratitude to the caretaker. This is the beginning schema for adoration and worship. The infant fixes its gaze on its mother and recognizes her as the source of food and comfort. The mother's consistency in providing for the child's needs teaches the child to trust. The child learns from the mother's facial expression the emotions of love, concern, reassurance, and disapproval. The child holds out its arms as an early form of showing that it values the mother and wants to hold and be held. Adoration and trust, as observed in the preverbal infant, are the beginnings of worship instilled in humanity by the Creator.

While writing, I reflected back on my experiences of adoration. Thoughts of my mother and grandmother in early childhood brought warmth and appreciation. I adored them for what they provided and for the acceptance shown of my Core identity. The behaviors modeled by Mother and Grandmother taught my Core self what I could expect from my Creator. It became the beginning to understand worship. They read from Egermeier's Bible Story Book[16] and commented in such a way that God's Word was imprinted on my heart at a very early age. The Creator is a true caretaker who delights in providing for our needs. As the child learns of God's love and provision for him or her, the child expresses adoration to God as one would to an earthly parent.

<u>Learning and Worship</u> — Learning about the world is a natural developmental behavior placed within every infant by the Creator. Jean Piaget, a French psychologist, studied how children acquired knowledge. Convinced that seeking knowledge was hard-wired into the human mind, Piaget called this ability "genetic epistemology."[17] He observed children going through a universal pattern of knowledge acquisition. When the child first <u>experienced </u>something new, the mind took notice and learned from the experience. For example, an infant being active while lying on its back will make random leg and arm movements. Suddenly, his arm passes in front of his face. The child becomes still for a few moments and then begins to move again. Once again, the arm moves across the child's field of vision. Again he stops. The second phase of acquiring knowledge is <u>assimilation.</u> The child begins to associate the external visual sensation

with an internal sensation from the muscles of the arm. As the child is able to create the movement and see the result, the child repeats the behavior frequently until that knowledge becomes part of the mental schema. Accommodation is the third stage of knowing evident by the child having the knowledge, using the knowledge appropriately, and being confident that it is available whenever needed.

Piaget also identified ages where different types of knowledge are incorporated. In the first two years of life, the child learns through sensing and doing. That simple concept of worship emerges from the child's interaction with the caretaker. From two to seven years of age, learning involves language and mental images. The child's view of the world in that stage is egocentric. What happens in the child's environment is seen as related directly to the child's circumstances. A black cat walks in front of the child on the way to school. On arrival at school, she cannot find her lunch money. The child sees the black cat is to blame. Breaking a mirror, walking under a ladder, spilling salt are seen as causes of misfortune. The superstitious person attempts to avert disaster by worship rituals—salt is thrown over the left shoulder, a black cat becomes a family pet, a broken mirror is ground to dust and scattered, ladders are avoided because it is sacrilege to walk through three-sided shapes which represents the Trinity and sacred ground. The naive perspective attempts to avoid tragedy by worship rituals meant to reduce the fear of misfortune.

Children between seven and twelve years of age use logic and organize thoughts into categories. The child thinks in terms of rules and wants both positive and negative consequences to be fair. If children are engaged in play, the child whose ball is used becomes the voice of reason. That child can assert the rules of the game. If his or her playmates disagree, the logical thing is to take the ball and go home. Children at this age can be like little Pharisees. Worship is characterized by obedience to or compliance with the rule maker and the one whose possessions are needed by the group. After twelve, the teenager can use scientific reasoning and create hypotheses to figure things out. The worship of mature thinkers involves an appreciation for the intangible. Mature thinkers recognize that not everything can be based solely on concrete, material evidence. Value can be assigned to the immaterial through faith as a factor. As the writer of Hebrews states, "Faith is the confidence that what we hope for will actually happen; it gives us assurance about things we cannot see." (Hebrews 11:1 NLT)

The Brain and Worship — Recent research in neurocognitive development indicates the role of mirror neurons in learning. As the child develops, a period of imitative learning or play helps the developing brain of the child to understand activities and emotions by mimicking the parent's behaviors and emotions. The little boy watches his father mowing the lawn or the little girl sees her mother vacuuming. The child finds an object he or she can push that then becomes the lawnmower or vacuum cleaner. The function of imitation is another expression of adoration and love toward the parent. The child who is not free to imitate does not learn empathy or understand the emotions of self and others. As the child learns and understands emotions by mirroring others, adoration from the child naturally follows. Imitating the parent is another origin of expressing worship. What parent is not pleased to see the child honor by imitation? Sadly, this is also the stage of life that children begin to associate language and emotion and may mimic the language and actions of the angry parent.

Stop for a moment. Does this stir you as it does me? How amazing is the Creator's design! These few examples show how the Creator's design for humanity to worship can be observed in the developing child. The developing mind of every child goes through these steps of growth. May we be aware of the influence we as adults can have on children and be intentional to influence them to worship as the Creator desires.

Hero and Celebrity Worship

Idolatry is a longstanding practice of humanity since Adam was sent from the Garden. Turning from worshiping the Creator to worshiping the creation showed the effects of Adam and Eve eating from the Wisdom Tree. Those who place value on any aspect of creation above that of the Creator show their mental and spiritual confusion. The Apostles Paul and John as the last writers of Scripture inspired by the Holy Spirit challenged believers to give God what He rightly deserved, acknowledging His preeminence over all creation.

"Yes, they knew God, but they wouldn't worship him as God or even give him thanks. And they began to think up foolish ideas of what God was like. As a result, their minds became dark and confused. Claiming to be wise, they instead became utter fools. And instead of worshiping the glorious, ever-living God, they worshiped idols made to look like mere people and birds and animals and reptiles." (Romans 1:21-23 NLT)

"And we know that the Son of God has come, and he has given us understanding so that we can know the true God. And now we live in fellowship with the true God because we live in fellowship with his Son, Jesus Christ. He is the only true God, and he is eternal life. Dear children, keep away from *(idols)* anything that might take God's place in your hearts." (1 John 5:20-21 NLT)

Worship that focuses on Creator God embodies hope for humanity; such focus requires the worshiper to see the evidence of the Creator's existence. The contemporary dilemma for humanity is to rely on the senses to find evidence for hope. Entertainment media provides a wealth of images and stories. If life is stark to an individual, identifying with a lead character compensates for anxiety, depression, and emptiness. The Relational self identifies with media figures and even shapes itself after them to find ways of coping with life stressors. Celebrity Worship Syndrome (CWS) came into public consciousness in 2003 when The Daily Mail of England released the article "Do You Worship Celebrities?" Defined as an obsessive compulsive or an addictive disorder, the effects of CWS was an area of study for media psychology researcher Stuart Fischoff, PhD.

Dr. Fischoff posed that the need to find an idol and follow him or her is programmed into the DNA of humanity. "What's in our DNA, as a social animal, is the interest in looking at alpha males and females; the ones who are important in the pack." Dr. Fischoff takes the evolutionary premise that the existing biochemical state of humanity makes us vulnerable to the spin doctors of Hollywood. Look at the emotional reactions of fans that follow a performer like Elvis Presley or a musical group like the Beatles. Long after their deaths, myths formed. Consider the sightings of Elvis Presley by those who refuse to believe that he died.

Contemporary performers and fans follow the same dynamics because this is the schema of worship. The goal to be close to and acknowledged by the idol becomes a driving passion. Attendance at every live concert is one means to connect with the idol. Being close to the stage to have a personal encounter or get an article of clothing allows the person to make the idol a close part of one's life like an intimate friend or family member. CWS can become problematic when an individual becomes so enmeshed in the life of a celebrity that he or she loses sight of reality.

One such case I witnessed was that of a very shy teenage girl. Raised in a very dysfunctional Christian family, Connie became enamored with the Beatles. Connie was first generation American whose parents were of British descent. To gain some recognition from her peers, Connie told her schoolmates that she was a cousin to Ringo Starr. Her stories grew in anticipation for the Beatles concert in Milwaukee, Wisconsin, on September 4th, 1964. Connie had built status with her schoolmates and was being recognized for the first time. Her fear of discovery and loneliness led her to tell others that while Ringo was in Milwaukee, he had sex with her and she was pregnant with his baby. Over the next four months, Connie displayed all the visible signs of pregnancy. She gained status among her peers. Connie's parents had medical follow-up for their daughter who was then 18 years old.

On a Sunday morning in January of 1965, Connie came to church with what appeared to be a baby wrapped in a blanket. She sat with her family quite proud of the birth. Remember that I said the family was quite dysfunctional? The parents were playing along with Connie who had a medical condition called pseudocyesis, or false pregnancy. Connie's mind had supported her narrative so that her body had all the symptoms of pregnancy. That Sunday morning, five months after the concert the false placenta let go and in Connie's mind she delivered her baby. The parents allowed Connie to continue her fantasy and bring a doll wrapped in a blanket as the baby she had by Ringo Starr. Sadly, Connie was institutionalized as was the practice of the time, and I heard no more of her story. CWS can leave people deeply wounded if they do not have a support network to help them sustain reality.

These ideas show evidence that worship is a natural expression of humanity from developmental behaviors to addictive patterns that seek to meet needs in an individual's life. This can happen when the Relational self is lost, confused, or enjoying fantasy. If we consider the energy and expense that people invest in the worship of fellow human beings, what range of expression could worship of the Creator really take. One verse stands out to me as what provokes true worship from the believer.

> You love him even though you have never seen him. Though you do not see him now, you trust him; and you rejoice with a glorious, inexpressible joy. The reward for trusting him will be the salvation of your souls. (1 Peter 1:8-9 NLT)

Our worship can be described as the delight of a childlike gaze into the Creator's eyes as He nurtures and cares for us. It is the expression of "Abba" that is equivalent to calling our Creator "Daddy or Dad" as we call upon Him in childlike faith with the confidence we are accepted by Him.

> So you have not received a spirit that makes you fearful slaves. Instead, you received God's Spirit when he adopted you as his own children. Now we call him, "Abba, Father." For his Spirit joins with our spirit to affirm that we are God's children. (Romans 8:15-16 NLT)

> And because we are his children, God has sent the Spirit of his Son into our hearts, prompting us to call out, "Abba, Father." Now you are no longer a slave but God's own child. And since you are his child, God has made you his heir. (Galatians 4:6-7 NLT)

Without intending to sound flippant or trite, Jesus Christ is our hero whom we rightfully worship since He rescued us from sin and death. In keeping with hero worship within the world, our desire is to be more like Him. We are encouraged and empowered by the Spirit of God for that transformation.

> For God knew his people in advance, and he chose them to become like his Son, so that his Son would be the firstborn among many brothers and sisters. (Romans 8:29 NLT)

> So all of us who have had that veil removed can see and reflect the glory of the Lord. And the Lord—who is the Spirit—makes us more and more like him as we are changed into his glorious image. (2 Corinthians 3:18 NLT)

> Dear friends, we are already God's children, but he has not yet shown us what we will be like when Christ appears. But we do know that we will be like him, for we will see him as he really is. (1 John 3:2 NLT)

Does your life and worship reflect that you are a child of God? Do you experience the amazement of that truth and subsequently express praise? Are you looking forward to the day when you experience Him with your senses, when you will see the scars of the nails in His hands and feet, the scars of the whip on His back, and of the thorns on His brow? That experience will not be a long lasting grief but become a triumphant expression to the praise of His Glory. Your voice and mine will join the myriads of redeemed humanity finally giving our Creator the long overdue expression of praise.

Neurotheology and the Study of Worship

Neurotheology is a new area of study that explores how the human mind experiences a range of spiritual experiences and expressions. For millennia, nothing has dissuaded human beings from thoughts of a divine being. Hypothetically, evolution-based science anticipates educated humanity no longer needing a concept of the divine.

Andrew Newberg is a neuroscientist who published "Principles of Neurotheology" to propose guidelines for integrative studies of neurology and theology. His principles allow a dialogue between these sciences rather than a continuation of the schism between religion and science. Throughout this series, I have sought to acquaint you with how science gives us a deeper insight into the magnificent work of our Creator. Newberg desires to keep this interchange open between scientific study of the brain and mind with the theological study of spirituality and religion. After decades of strict material science, Newberg challenges that view with two books: "How God Changes the Brain" and "Why God Won't Go Away." These scholarly treatises represent the integration of science and theology. From this premise, we will briefly explore neurotheological concepts regarding worship.

Alexis Abernethy, Professor of Psychology at Fuller Theological Seminary is the editor of the book, "Worship that Changes Lives." This collection of articles explores a range of ideas about theological and experiential aspects of worship. Professor Abernethy described worship as a transforming experience in which the Holy Spirit minis- ters deep within the person seeking an encounter with God. Other arti- cles in the book grapple with how the arts enhance corporate worship by means of drama, dance, readings, and music; how worship could be a daily life experience rather than based on one weekly service; and how the narrative of the worshiper can give clues to improving the worship. What I gleaned from her book was that worship builds a personal relationship with Creator God, produces transformation as that relationship is internalized, gives evidence of spiritual matu- rity, and helps the worshiper face rather than avoid stress, disquiet, and suffering in life.

Rev. Barbara White, minister at Bedford Park United in Toronto believes that theological schools need to add neurocognitive studies to seminary curricula. This area of study would seek means to facil- itate corporate worship, including more of the congregation in each experience. White is quoted, "I deeply believe that this is where worship should go. This is how worship could work. Worship is not education. It is an authentic experience of an encounter with the holy. The goal is to inspire." Her comments are consistent with St. Augustine of Hippo from the Third Century. Augustine held that the purpose of preaching was to teach, inspire, and delight. His desire was to provoke worship of God by awakening delight in his audi- ence. Does your pastor provoke you to delight in God, Jesus Christ, and/or the Holy Spirit? That is what Barbara White wishes ministers would learn; how to provoke delight in God which naturally promotes worship.

Other studies on worship demonstrate amazing changes in human health that take place in the human brain. Meditation that focuses on gratitude to God for His gifts to us, contemplation on the compassion the Father shows us through the offering of His Son, and awareness that when we were without hope Jesus died for us actually increases the density of brain gray matter. This further affirms the findings of neural plasticity. Intentional mindfulness prepares us for worship by the simple awareness of our breath. Our breath verifies our Core existence. The Creator formed us in His image, breathed us alive, and gave us a soul. By being in the moment, focusing on one's breath, letting go of judgmental thoughts, and releasing feelings that intrude on that moment of peace, gives our Core being a sense of the Creator's presence. Mindful worship keeps us in the present moment rather than becoming lost in our historical past. Christ died once in the historical past about 2100 years ago. The present day impact of the death of Christ brings us to experience the power of His atonement and forgiveness in the present moment of worship. The redemptive work of Christ transcends time and space. Experiencing that truth through worship is truly transforming.

The parietal lobe of the right hemisphere of the brain is one area of the brain that assists in producing positive emotions. If that area of the brain is damaged or neurochemically depleted, a person is inconsolable. Comfort and other positive feelings are difficult to experience. Worship in the presence of supportive people in a faith community invites us to experience comfort and peaceful feelings. Corporate worship retrains the brain circuitry in the inconsolable. Reinforcement by continued worship opportunities allows the individual to build new pathways in the brain so the individual can experience consolation and, even more incredible, experience other positive feelings. Isn't it amazing that the way we were hardwired by our Creator to express worship and awe is also a major force in the healing and ongoing health of our mind, body, and soul?

Don't be surprised if you arrive at a church service one day to find three strangers with clipboards spread throughout the congregation. From the moment they enter the building, each is in the field study of worship in your church, busily making checkmarks on a survey sheet. Questions were asked such as: Did the minister, the worship leader, the worship team, and/or the congregants participate? Were there spontaneous unplanned behaviors? How did people feel about the location of worship, the number of people in attendance, and the type of music used? What actions were seen as related to worship? Behaviors were recorded such as the frequency of raised hands, body positions like sitting, standing, or kneeling during singing or prayer, liturgical or spontaneous dance, singing by choir, vocalist, or congregant. Emotions were observed and changes noted according to chronological time in the service.

Sensory data like room temperature, physical space between congregants, types and intensity of odors, sounds levels, types of musical instruments, and the styles of music were collected. Participants answered questionnaires and interviews to share their thoughts and reactions to worship and how they were impacted by the experience. Hopefully, all the data collected could help explain the quality of the worship experience and provide insight into enhanced corporate worship. This would be neurotheological research into what might enhance the worship expression to the glory of God. You or someone you know might be disturbed by this scientific attitude present in a church worship service. Some would say this stifles or hinders the Holy Spirit. Please consider that the outcome of these observations may help believers mature in faith and fulfill the Spirit's directive to support unity in the body of Christ.

> Let us hold tightly without wavering to the hope we affirm, for God can be trusted to keep his promise. Let us think of ways to motivate one another to acts of love and good works. And let us not neglect our meeting together, as some people do, but encourage one another, especially now that the day of his return is drawing near. (Hebrews 10:23-25 NLT)

Neurotheology may bring a greater understanding and amazement of the Creator's handiwork leading to a Core expression of praise to our Creator as we await His return to take us to the new creation He is preparing. Heaven and earth as we know it will be gone.

But you and I will be changed into His likeness and worship Him as intended in that new Heaven and Earth. We will finally experience His Sabbath Rest of the seventh day.

Core Consciousness and Worship

The focus of this series, <u>Coming to Awe, Finding Identity</u>, seeks to encourage you to live as your Creator intended. His desire was that we worship Him from our Core being. Through the redeeming work of His Son, our Core being is restored, is able to experience loving kindness, and seeks through worship to express gratitude. To enhance your awe regarding the Creator's design, we are going to search Core consciousness as related to worship. Six areas of awareness define core consciousness in any present moment by means of the acronym BASK-VE: Behavior, Affect, Sensation, Knowledge, Volition, and Energy.

The Apostle Paul pled with Roman believers to worship God from their Core being. The passage in Romans 12 provides an excellent framework to explore these consciousness components in the context of worship. In this passage, conscious worship is expressed by a material being to the non-material Creator through each component. Let's examine this passage from the scientific perspective of human consciousness that reflects the image of God. You will find each of the BASK-VE components of consciousness are present. The superscript letters indicate which of consciousness components are present.

> And so, dear brothers and sisters, I plead^{B,A,E} with you to give^V your bodies^{B,S} to God because of all he has done for you.^{K,E} Let^V them be a living^E and holy$^{BASK-VE}$ sacrifice^{B,S}—the kind he will find acceptable.$^{BASK-VE}$ This is truly the way^B to worship him.^{A,K} Don't copy^{V,E} the behavior^K and customs^{A,S} of this world, but let^V God transform^{K,V,E} you into a new person^E by changing the way you think^K. Then you will learn^K to know God's will for you, which is good^{A,K,E} and pleasing^{A,S} and perfect.^{K} (Romans 12:1-2 NLT)

The following key is a guide to where the different components of consciousness manifest aspects of Core conscious worship.

Behavior — *[Transformed Actions]* The actions of worship do not mimic this world's behavior.

Affect — *[Good* (holy in intent) *and Pleasing* (what God desires) *and Perfect* (complete in expression)*]* Worship means active, intentional gratitude expressed to God for the gift of His Son.

Sensation — *[With your body]* Worship requires the use of your physical body by means of your senses and your actions.

Knowledge — *[Change the way you think]* Worship transforms thinking in ways that makes you different from the secular world.

Volition — *[Give your body as your sacrifice]* Worship is intentional commitment to use your body only in ways that please and honor God.

Energy — *[A New Person]* Worship results in following God's plan in your life, finding joy and peace beyond measure, and becoming renewed and refreshed.

Paul wants every believer to think of worship as an expression that is rooted in physicality. Paul begs us as believers to dedicate our bodies to God because of what He did for us through Jesus Christ. He challenges us to give our physical bodies as the instrument to express our worship. The material body where your Core being dwells is your instrument of worship to be dedicated to the Creator. He made you a living soul inhabiting a material body to express praise. God's word does not tell us how to worship. We are to just worship! As you have come to realize in this chapter, I believe that humanity was hardwired for worship by the Creator. Gratitude is just one means and one reason to worship and praise Him for who He is.

When Paul wrote to the Church at Corinth, he cautioned them from misusing Christian liberty. Some rationalized that because God created physical organs that we should have the right to use them as we see fit. For example, since God gave us a stomach to enjoy food, we should be free to enjoy eating. The danger is that in our humanity, our Relational self can fall prey to overindulgence. Based on that premise, some claim freedom in sexual behavior. Such practices are hedonistic worship that focuses on creation not on the Creator. The Holy Spirit indwells our bodies as a holy place, a temple, a place of worship. Christ paid a high price to redeem us and transform us from objects of debase slavery into vessels of holy worship. Awareness that God indwells us brings us to realize that we belong to God and wish to honor Him for the price He paid and the suffering He endured to redeem us.

> Don't you realize that your bodies are actually parts of Christ? Should a man take his body, which is part of Christ, and join it to a prostitute? Never! And don't you realize that if a man joins himself to a prostitute, he becomes one body with her? For the Scriptures say, "The two are united into one." But the person who is joined to the Lord is one spirit with him.

> Run from sexual sin! No other sin so clearly affects the body as this one does. For sexual immorality is a sin against your own body. Don't you realize that your body is the temple of the Holy Spirit, who lives in you and was given to you by God? You do not belong to yourself, for God bought you with a high price. So you must honor God with your body. (1 Corinthians 6:15-18 NLT)

Core consciousness brings us to realize the immense price Jesus Christ paid to redeem us and bring us back to God. Worship is the least we can give in return. That worship involves all of our consciousness. The following is an attempt to encapsulate all these aspects of consciousness into a worship description. Worship is an expression of the heart[A], energized by our Core being[E], displayed through our actions[B], directed by our knowledge of our Creator[K], with the intent[V] to praise Him[S] for all that He has accomplished for us[S].

The actions of worship are difficult to define precisely. Some see worship as singing; some as reading scripture; still others as attending a church service and listening to a sermon. I like Abernethy's defi-nition of worship as "a transforming experience by which the Holy Spirit ministers deep within the person seeking an encounter with God." These words sound idealistic from a human standpoint — an encounter with God. Following a testimony to the transforming power of Christ in one man's life, men gathered around a wooden cross. On a near-by table were pieces of paper, pens, square nails, and a four pound sledgehammer. Anyone who had thoughts and feelings of bitterness, resentment, hurt, loneliness, or rejection could write out those thoughts on a piece of paper and nail the paper to the cross. This symbolic activity produced quiet worship punctuated with sounds of hammering, prayers of confession, and heartfelt sobs of men encoun-tering the loving kindness of the Eternal God, some for the first time. This example was an integration of personal and corporate worship. All present witnessed the transforming power of the Spirit of God.

✍ *Journal Time – What is Your Experience of Worship?*

Consider writing out your experiences of worship. How do you prepare for worship? Where and at what times do you worship? What brought you to sense the presence of God? How does your private worship compare to corporate worship? How does your expression of worship transform you?

Chapter 7

MATURING THROUGH WORSHIP

How I Learned to Worship

This is the narrative of my journey to learn to worship. Through these encounters my Core being became free to exist, experience, and express my relationship with God. I hope that my narrative may lead you to be mindful of intentional worship that you will express often. May you encounter the transforming evidence of the Holy Spirit at work in your Core being through your worship. The hymns referred to in this narrative are referenced to Internet sites for specific hymnbooks that should be available on line for a long time. The sources of the worship lyrics used in this chapter are listed in the End Notes. In preparation for this study, I encourage you to use the links there to access these hymns on line. Print them out for your personal use. Read the hymn lyrics when they appear in this chapter as a means to experience and express worship together.

I was raised in a small church with a congregation of 50 people in Cudahy, Wisconsin. My church attendance began in my second week of life. Church attendance consisted of two services on Sunday morning — Sunday school where adults and children attended classes based on age and topic and Family Bible Hour, which was a preaching service. Sunday evening was the worship service called "The Lord's Supper." Wednesday night was prayer meeting and Bible study that consisted of thirty minutes of prayer for the health and welfare of congregants, the needs of missionaries, the concerns in our country and the world, and thirty minutes of scriptural teaching. This church routine continued after my father moved the family to Lake Geneva when I was 13 years of age where he began to work in children's ministry. The Lake Geneva church was also small with ethnic variety and the spiritual practices were the same.

The Cudahy neighborhood consisted of a variety of ethnic groups who worked in nearby industries—Patrick Cudahy Pork Processors, the Bucyrus Erie Company, the Ladish Drop Forge Plant, and the Peter Cook Animal Hide Glue Factory in nearby Carrolville. The diversity of the area was reflected in the church membership—British, Irish, Russian, Polish, Swiss, Mexican American, Slavic, and German immigrants either first or second-generation whose English was heavily accented with occasional relapses into their native tongue. Fourth generation Americans were the minority of which I was one.

My mother and father were raised in this same church. My father was raised in poverty a few blocks from the church. The church provided him men of character as healthy social and spiritual examples. The care shown to the children of the neighborhood had a long-standing benefit in those who continued in faith. Many of the men of the church came back after World War II to jobs that paid well so they could live away from the poverty. Church attendance continued to that so they could leave a spiritual legacy as was left with them. They followed the men of faith who mentored them by reaching out to the children in that impoverished area to teach them of God's love.

My mother's parents lived away from the area during the Depression. Pop Orloff worked at Bucyrus Erie as an engineer and Mom Orloff took in twenty-one foster children during the Depression and World War II years. Milwaukee County Welfare Offices were in need of loving homes to care for these hurting kids. Through that small church, children spanning four decades learned of the love of God and came to faith in Christ. I also learned of Jesus in that environment.

The liturgical practices in the church were what some would see as rather primitive and unfamiliar. Instrumental music was only used in the Family Bible Hour. Mr. Brauch, another engineer, was an accomplished musician who would lead the singing with a saxophone dangling from a strap around his neck. Granny Fadel accompanied on the upright piano. When the spirit moved, Mr. Brauch would begin to play the sax, picking up the tempo of the hymns being sung.

The Sunday evening service was typically considered the worship service that the elders called "The Lord's Supper." This was based on the Last Supper when Christ broke bread with his disciples in the upper room on Passover. All agreed that since it was referred to as "supper," it had to be held on Sunday evening. Faithfully, at 7:30 PM, those in attendance would sit in one of two rows of chairs that encircled a simple table where there were three objects: a plate with an uncut loaf of bread, a cup filled with wine, and a basket for one's tithe. The outer circle was for the children and for anyone in attendance who had not made a profession of faith in Christ. The inner circle was for those who would participate in communion. To qualify to take communion, one made a profession of faith in Christ and was baptized. Each worshiper in the inner circle had a small hymnbook and their Bible they would refer throughout the hour long service.

The hymnbook was titled "Hymns and Spiritual Songs for the Little Flock."[18] The first publication was in 1881 and had been changed little since. There were no musical notes in the book, just chords, meter, and sol-fa references. No instrumental music was used at the Lord's Supper. The melodies were known by heart or a substitute melody was used according to the hymn's meter. Mr. Brauch was relied upon to begin each requested song in the right key with all singing done a cappella. The remainder of the worshipers would join in by the end of the first phrase. (This church group was of the belief that women were to be silent in the worship service. They could sing but they could not pray, read scripture, or share a thought aloud.)

I grew up with this style and practice of worship, understanding this was done in obedience to Jesus who asked His disciples to remember Him in His death, burial, and resurrection until He returned to take them to Heaven. Until His return, He was preparing our dwelling place in Heaven. The hour was marked with prayer that praised the Father for sending His Son to redeem us, that exalted Christ for his atoning work, and that acknowledged the Holy Spirit for sustaining us by His indwelling. Scripture was read relating to the atoning work of Christ. Hymns were selected to express the theme that emerged through the corporate expression of worship.

The imagery in the lyrics of those old hymns created for me a powerful sense of God's work and His presence. No service was ever the same. Sure, there were some who had their favorite hymns that you knew if they spoke which hymn they would request. But even those requests seemed to dovetail with a central theme around the work of Christ unique to that evening.

At nine years of age, I answered the Elders' questions about the meaning of salvation, baptism, and communion. After I was baptized, I was invited to sit in the innermost circle where those who partook of communion sat. Forty-five minutes were spent in prayer, reading, singing, and shared thoughts from God's Word on the person and work of Christ. Every expression focused on the person of Christ and His work. During that time, no one prayed for missionaries, a troubled son or daughter, the need to find a job, and so on. The sole focus was on praising, thanking, and glorifying God for the sacrifice of His Son. The whole time was about a sacrifice of praise, giving thanks to His name for the salvation He provided for us. It was about praising God for His personal care extended through His Son. There were times of silent contemplation as well.

The hymn lyrics reflected a depth of meaning that taught about the different aspects of Christ's death. One worship theme was on the adequacy of His shed blood offered once at Calvary. This contrasted to hundreds of years of sacrifices by the patriarchs and the prophets at their stone altars in the presence of Jehovah. With the Exodus came the tabernacle and the Aaronic priesthood began. The Jewish priests officiating in the Tabernacle, then in Solomon's Temple, and later in Herod's Temple slaughtered many animals over the centuries with the intent to sacrifice to Jehovah to atone for the sin of the worshiper. Passages were read illustrating a redemptive theme from Scripture. Lyrics written in 1709 were sung to a melody with musical timing that led to deep contemplation on the hymn writer's words. The message of the hymn was in the first few words: "Not all the blood of beasts on Jewish altars slain, could give the guilty conscience peace or wash away the stain."[19]

Another theme was the alienation that Christ experienced on our behalf. There is a deep theological concept expressed in these lyrics in relation to the Holy of Holies in the Tabernacle. The High Priest was the only one allowed in the Holy of Holies behind the veil of the Temple and then only after careful preparation. When he entered, it was with a rope tied to him so if he had overlooked anything in preparation to enter God's presence and died upon entering God's presence, his body could be pulled out from behind the veil. By the work of Christ, a believer has free access to enter the Holy of Holies through the atonement of Christ that makes us holy before God. "Through Thy precious body broken inside the veil"[20] speaks to Jesus Christ being our High Priest who entered the Holy of Holies to atone for us. He was the perfect sacrifice for our sin because He was fully human yet without sin.

When He hung on the cross of Calvary dying in your place and mine, the Father turned away from Him as He bore our sin. In that moment, the veil of the Temple was ripped from top to bottom. Imagine the high priest standing in front of that veil, the rope tied around his waist, prepared to enter the Holy of Holies, and suddenly the thick veil is open, he is seeing into that place he dare not enter but once each year. This same high priest held court just hours before condemning Jesus for blasphemy. He wasn't at the cross because protocol required him to officiate in the Holy place at that moment. All the venom he had spewed at Jesus in his self-righteous rage the previous evening surely was turned to weak-kneed terror in that moment.

Another time the theme might be looking beyond the cross and the grave to worship Him for His incomparable worth. "Come, let us sing the matchless worth"[21] brings our worship to His shining glory witnessed by Israel when Moses came from the presence of God and also the glory that shined from Jesus witnessed by Peter, James, and John on the Mount of Transfiguration. The image that came to mind was how I might reflect the glory of Christ after being in His presence in worship. Would others sense something different about me because I was in His presence in worship?

When there were about 15 minutes remaining, one of the men would stand and approach "The Lord's Table" and pray. That prayer expressed thanksgiving for the loaf of bread that symbolized the physical body of Christ, perfect God in human form who bore our sins in His body on the Cross of Calvary. The loaf of bread was broken open symbolizing His body broken for us. The broken loaf of bread was passed with each person tearing off a piece of bread, passing the plate on to the next person to do the same. Head bowed in meditative thought, the piece of bread was eaten while contemplating that through His sinless being we who were sinners were made holy by his physical death and resurrection.

When the plate was returned to the table, another man would stand and pray thanking God that by the shedding of Christ's blood we were washed clean. The deepest stain of sin was washed whiter than snow. The cup of wine was passed with each person taking a sip and meditating on the cleansing blood of Christ. When the cup arrived at the last person, it was placed on the table. The offering basket was passed around the circle and then placed on the table. A closing song and or prayer ended the service. Things returned to normal conversation. I would feel a twinge in my gut at times wondering how people could change so suddenly from thoughts of worshiping God to making plans for the week ahead.

Before long, I as a child began to notice uniqueness to each service. Something miraculous was at work. I started to recognize worship as more than what some saw and heard in that service which could be seen as predictable by the type of activity: pray, sing, read, preach, partake of the emblems. Something deeper was at work that could only come from the Spirit of God. At least I knew that to be my experience. I knew God was close in those moments.

From my youth, I witnessed the Spirit of God at work in ordinary men and women. Simple men without any theological training yet highly educated in their professions like agribusiness, engineering, manufacturing, and business management read God's word and studied with a seminarian's passion. In sitting around that communion table with the focus on the work of Christ, and His life, death, burial, and resurrection, I heard from each one how alive and real God was to them.

Brother Jacob Kratt, a wise old farmer, would begin to pray. "Lord, how amazing you are that you went to the cross on my behalf. I am such a wretch, as you know. I am so undeserving of your love.

I am a worm, an undeserving creature. Yet you loved me enough to withstand the stripes that the whip ploughed on your back; the crown of thorns was pressed deep into your brow so blood flowed down your face; and the jeering words used by the Roman soldiers in their mockery of who you were. You bore the humiliation of being spit upon. Your disciples abandoned you. Even your Father in that darkest hour could not look upon you because of my sin which you bore on that cross." That tough elderly German in his thick German accent had such a graphic verbal depiction of the crucifixion that the words of his prayer created a vivid image in my mind of Christ at the mercy of the Roman soldiers and the crowd. The images were cemented there in my mind by the tears on his face. Yes, I opened my eyes and looked when people prayed. My hearing impairment from birth required that I read lips to hear what was said. My eyes listened to expressive worship first hand.

I would find myself singing the songs during the week. On one occasion, my father ran a newly installed stop sign and was caught by a policeman who turned on his siren and waved my father over. Dad agreed to follow the officer to the police station to pay the ticket. The parking lot for the police station was in the alley. The car windows were down on that warm summer evening. At seven years of age, I was bored while waiting so I began to sing.

The reason I picked the particular song may have been totally coincidental. With the gusto I was known for, I sang "At the Cross," all six verses, unaware that my voice wafted through the open window into the room with the sergeant's desk. I later heard my father chuckling as he told my mother how my voice came through the police station window loudly and clearly as I sang, "Was it for crimes that I have done He groaned upon the tree? Amazing pity! Grace unknown! And love beyond decree!"[22] Out of the mouths of babes, God ordains wisdom, but also <u>worship</u>.

My teenage Relational self found it difficult to speak out during worship because it was in front of family. Beginning at fifteen years of age I would preach in Family Bible Hour being mentored by our pastor, but that was different than worship. When I was in college, I began to speak and pray during worship. My spirit was stirred by themes I heard from scriptures read, hymns sung, and prayers offered.

Verses came to mind that stirred my heart and brought me to awe as I reflected on the work of Christ.

At times, I felt like my heart would burst if I didn't share what I was learning from that time of worship. What motivated me to speak was not recognition from others. I wanted others to join my awe. This book has been a microcosm of my excitement to share with you how amazing our Lord and Savior is. I want people to join in worship with the focus on the person of Jesus Christ and His work. In fact as I wrote this narrative of my worship experience, one hymn kept going through my Core being. I am so thankful to the Lord Jesus for all He has done for you and me that I wish you could sing with me the words to the hymn, "A thousand, a thousand thanksgivings, I bring blessed Savior to thee."[23] The message acknowledges that Jesus was our source of life by dying for us when we were the ones who deserved death. What was rightfully our punishment and suffering, He took for us out of love and empathic grief so that we would be eternally free. As the title alludes we are compelled to give our blessed Lord a thousand thanksgivings. In fact that will be one of the ongoing events in eternity.

My worship experience led me to believe that real worship consists of simple components—a focus on Jesus Christ in His life, death, burial, resurrection, and ascension; an obedience to His expressed desire that we remember Him often; a reminder of His body broken and blood shed symbolized by the bread and wine; an attitude of anticipation that He may return at anytime to call us to be with Him for eternity; and a passion to worship Him as an expression of gratitude for His atoning work that brought us to God.

Instrumental music and modern lyrics can enhance worship with thoughtful lyrics. Dancing with joy, falling to our knees in adoration, lifting our hands with praise may be physical gestures that express the state of the heart. Scripture reading and a sermon may teach the listener more about God. All can set the stage for a time of worship. However, as a faith community we need to provoke one another to awe at the many facets by which He demonstrated the Father's amazing love for us.

✍ Journal Time –How Does My Story Bring You to Worship?

Every Human Being Worships

If worship involves adoration and devotion or expressed love and demonstrated loyalty, then humanity worships numerous persons, places, and things. However, the intent of worship is deeper than a material value we assign to that person or object to which we feel devotion. There is an existential component. In our very being, in our human essence, we seek to be acknowledged by others. When someone or something acknowledges our existence, it arouses a sense of gratitude toward that person or object. But is that person or object deserving of true worship? A pet can be very affirming; a cat, a dog, a bird, a horse—each may show us appreciation and adoration.

But while a pet that acknowledges our existence is nice, worship is only deserved for someone who sustains our existence. If you were suffering in the midst of a life-threatening crisis and your life had been saved by a physician, an EMT, or even a neighbor, you would find yourself feeling a debt of gratitude toward that person. Often the voice of gratitude says, "I owe you my life." Hence the belief in some cultures that one is forever indebted to the person who saved them. The Talmud, Sanhedrin 37a indicates the far-reaching importance of an act of saving a life:

> "For this reason was man created alone, to teach thee that whosoever destroys a single soul... scripture imputes [guilt] to him as though he had destroyed a complete world; and whosoever preserves a single soul..., scripture ascribes [merit] to him as though he had preserved a complete world."

Now put this in the context of your Core being, that which is central to your identity. Who is most deserving of your gratitude? Do you believe that you are your own creator? By your education and experience, by the abilities you have and use (maybe even for the betterment of humanity) do you take the credit for your success? Those who adopt that attitude tend to expect worship from others.

Is there someone you look to that is supernatural, beyond time and space, an ultimate source of hope, a sustaining force or power?

He who saved your life was present at the right time in human history. But how did they happen to be available, at the precise moment when you were in need? Was it karma? Fate? Luck? If you view the world in that manner, you give credit to scientific or mathematical probability or you uphold fate or chance to sustain you.

Humanity derives a sense of hope in what humanity values as divine by nature and deserving of praise. In the old English definition, that which we value as the source of what sustains us is deserving of our "worth"-ship. To praise one's self, to give credit to science, to ascribe our fortuitous outcomes to cosmic chance is to say that these are what you value as divine or supernatural. Worshiping these things may seem easier than to give credit to a personal Creator who intimately desires a relationship with humanity and, more specifically – with you. But when a person experiences awe at the timing of events in their life, isn't it possible that this could point to a personal God who knows each of us in our Core being and loves us? Indeed, that same Creator desires a relationship with each individual whom He has created.

> "He is the God who made the world and everything in it. Since he is Lord of heaven and earth, he doesn't live in man-made temples, and human hands can't serve his needs—for he has no needs. He himself gives life and breath to everything, and he satisfies every need. From one man he created all the nations throughout the whole earth. He decided beforehand when they should rise and fall, and he determined their boundaries.

> "His purpose was for the nations to seek after God and perhaps feel their way toward him and find him—though he is not far from any one of us. For in him we live and move and exist." (Acts 17:24-28 NLT)

✎ *Journal Time—Who Do You Worship?*
To what or to whom do you credit positive events in your life?
To whom and how do you show or express gratitude?
What makes the object of your gratitude qualified to receive your adoration?

✍ *Journal Time Ends — Who Do You Worship?*

Existing to Worship

Core self, that personal aspect of our being that is associated with our birth name, is our focus in this final chapter exploring awe and identity. It is from Core consciousness that we have and hold that sense of "I" that we claim as our identity. Only in our Core being do we place value on our personal existence.

Our Relational being is primarily related to our interactions with others. The rules and roles that become familiar in social settings provide structure, cohesion, boundaries, and other guidelines for social functioning within our social contexts. Relational identity does not contemplate the spiritual in the general flow of social life. The more integration between our Core being and our Relational identity, the more our Core identity, Core values, and social responsiveness will be expressed with consistency. The more we live with our Core being as executive in life, the greater sense of harmony we will experience with others. The fact that a shared truth is known about each of us allows for continuity in many facets of life.

Creeds, catechisms, and statements of faith in many Christian traditions reflect two commonly shared beliefs regarding the purpose for humanity as God's creation. First, each individual human being is to give the Creator praise, glory, worship, and adoration from his Core being. Second, each individual is to sustain an ongoing mutually enjoyable relationship with the Creator. He has demonstrated through the work of Jesus, the Son of God, to be the Sustainer of our very existence, the Provider of all of our needs, and the Restorer of our once alienated soul.

When we recognize that our Creator could have wiped out all of His creation and started over again, we cannot help but marvel in awe, recognizing that our Creator genuinely loves us. We were not some flawed creative expression that the potter deemed inadequate or an error in His handiwork. Remember, He declared humanity "very good," the pièce de résistance of all His work. After forming the clay shape on His wheel, the potter did not discard it or reshape it to start again. He formed humanity in perfection with a clear purpose. He used His own image as the template for humanity's consciousness. Then, He declared His handiwork as "very good!"

Since we were made from the template of His own image, the template retains its integrity, able to stand the test of time. The flaw came because of Adam and Eve's disobedience resulting in a spiritual birth defect passed on to every subsequent generation. When Jesus, the Second Adam, came and died on the cross, spiritual gene therapy was provided. By faith in Jesus–who lived a life without sin, who died unjustly in humanity's stead, who was buried and then rose again, and who ascended to the Father's right hand to make preparations for us to join Him—humanity was provided the cure for this sin flaw. A child of wrath, by the power of faith in Jesus Christ, experiences the transformation of spiritual gene therapy. He or she becomes a child of God, is immediately an heir of promise, and becomes a new creation through Christ.

The apostle John wrote of the prognosis of those who have benefitted from this spiritual gene therapy.

See how very much our Father loves us, for he calls us his children, and that is what we are! But the people who belong to this world don't recognize that we are God's children because they don't know him. Dear friends, we are already God's children, but he has not yet shown us what we will be like when Christ appears. But we do know that we will be like him, for we will see him as he really is. And all who have this eager expectation will keep themselves pure, just as he is pure. (1 John 3:1-3 NLT)

The apostle Peter gives another diagnostic indicator of some Christians whose early faith experience had faltered. Peter wrote,

But those who fail to develop in this way are shortsighted or blind, forgetting that they have been cleansed from their old sins. (2 Peter 1:9 NLT)

When our Core being comes to fully realize the extent of God's love, we become aware that God continued to love us in spite of our alienation and hostility. Peter addresses the struggle that some young believers have, especially if they come to Christ due to social pressures.

The Core self must be involved in the choice. The unfathomable love of God manifested through the cross of Christ, will bring our Core self to stunned amazement that God must have truly loved us, His rebellious creation, to go to that extreme. John adds in the following passage the gripping reality that the only way that we even know love is because He loved us first.

> Such love has no fear, because perfect love expels all fear. If we are afraid, it is for fear of punishment, and this shows that we have not fully experienced his perfect love. We love each other because he loved us first. (1 John 418-19 NLT)

One who matches Peter's description in 1 Peter 1:9 is one who has not yet come to fully grasp within his or her Core being the totality of Jesus' redemptive act and the expense Jehovah God incurred to redeem us to Himself. This truth is the awe that brings one to worship and is the rationale from which one brings praise and glory to Him.

✍ *Journal Time—How Did You First Realize You Were to Worship?*

Experiencing Worship

All the features of consciousness that we have considered are the components that we bring to the experience of worship. The more components we use, either individually or as a faith community, the richer the experience of worship will be. Let's summarize the aspects available to the experience.

The BASK-VE model provides structure to any conscious experience. The identity piece describes the aspect of our identity that is consciously participating in the worship experience. If we worship to merely conform to what is expected as part of the social experience of church, we are worshiping from our Relational self not our Core self. A symptom of such worship is a lack of focus on our object of worship, our Creator. Such a worshiper observes others around them and may be critical of their behaviors. They may judge others'

179

mannerisms in worship as wrong or distracting such as lifting of hands or swaying in time with the music.

By contrast, if worship is personally important to you and you can be present with others without feeling self-conscious, you are more likely to be experiencing worship from Core consciousness. The benefit of this degree of awareness is that it may allow you to experience Him whom you value and seek. It may also make your worship even more intentional and meaningful to God.

In the following journal activity, I challenge you to become mindful of how you experience worship. Do you believe that God would also find what you seek to experience as appropriate, meaningful, and/or true worship? Give your Core self the freedom to rethink what you wish your experience of worship to be. The worship you experience can be both a private and a shared experience. You may worship without awareness of others around or your worship may be a consciously, non-judgmental sharing of worship with your faith community. However, in either case, remember your experience is intended to worship Jehovah, the Core Being of God, who of course is the only one worthy of our worship.

✍ *Journal Time—What Is Your Idea of Core Worship?*

Behavior—Consider worship in the traditions with which you are familiar. What does worship involve in the traditions you know? List the behaviors that you believe to be a part of the worship-related experience.

Affect—Is emotion a part of worship? If so, When, What, Who, Why, and How do emotions manifest? Are there emotions that don't belong in worship?

Sensation—The three primary senses are auditory, visual, and kinesthetic. What needs to be heard for one to experience worship? What visual images are part of worship? What are physical feelings or kinesthetic sensations in worship? How intentional is the kinesthetic experience of worship?

Knowledge—What beliefs are a basis for experiencing worship? Is worship a time for learning? What did Jesus mean by worshiping God in spirit and in truth? Are there any aspects that absolutely must be present for worship to be a complete experience?

Volition—What is your intent behind experiencing worship? Must you worship? What choices determine that your experience was meaningful? Pleasant? Satisfactory? Regretful? Do you consciously pay attention to the moment? Do you or can you ignore distractions? Why do you want to worship (if you do)?

Energy—What is the impact on your personal energy when experiencing worship? How often does the experience of worship impact your energy? What might have been involved in an experience of worship that exhausted you? Or, that energized you?

✍ *Journal Time Ends—What Is Your Idea of Core Worship?*

Expressing Conscious Worship

Nothing can compare to expressing yourself from your Core being. It is the most mindfully conscious state and has all the components that John Kabat-Zinn defines as a complete mindful experience: "paying attention, on purpose, in the moment, without judgment."

In the 1970s, while teaching at BlackHawk College, I would hear of students enamored with Transcendental Meditation (TM). The practice of TM was one where the meditator was to empty his mind so that he could enter a peaceful state. On occasion, the meditator would use a sound that lacked meaning as a way to focus, thereby creating a state of nothingness that was purported to bring peace. Throughout the years since that time, I have encountered those who continued to practice TM. What I found greatly disturbing is the lack of self in some who kept faithfully meditating. Even more alarming is that some of these individuals were quite often depressed and socially withdrawn from friends and family though they continued to practice TM. They lacked any distinct Core identity.

My conclusion was that these chronic meditators had become addicted to TM as a means to having a "blank" mind. The mental state of "mindlessness" felt safer. I found chronic TM users often had a trauma history, like veterans returning from Vietnam. The altered states of consciousness discovered in the 1960s were the resources to deal with the pain of the unmentionable. TM was available through higher education. It was an alternative to illegal drugs. It became a means to silence the intrusive thoughts, feelings, and images by having an empty mind. While some TM meditators adopted a social persona to define how they were known, TM meditators in particular seemed to have no defining personal identity and no energy to invest in relationships.

Expressing worship to Jehovah God fills our being with the reality of His presence, with praise for His plan, and with awe for His loving kindness. Mindful worship of the Creator provides an alternative to silencing mental pain and suffering. The Creator hardwired humanity to find healing of pain and suffering through true worship. Jesus sat at Jacob's well near the town of Sychar in Samaria. There He met a Samaritan woman who recognized Him as a Jew. She was surprised when He asked her for a drink. In the ensuing conversation, she asked Jesus where the right place to worship was, in Jerusalem or at Mount Gerizim in Samaria. Jesus replied to her,

> "True worshipers will worship the Father in spirit and in truth.
> the Father is looking for those who will worship him that
> way." (John 4:23 NLT)

Jesus answered this woman's questions with worshipful truth and led her Core identity out from under the shame that bound her Relational self. Through Jesus Christ, her Core being was awakened to worship not in a place or a manner but from within. Her Relational self focused externally on how others perceived her. Jesus who knew the reality of her life awakened her to listen to the Spirit of God and worship with Core expression. As the woman's Core being encountered the Messiah, she experienced the well of water springing up within her spirit. Jesus, the source of the wellspring within her, became the rightful focus of worship as she went into town.

As a true worshiper, she called the whole town to come worship at the feet of the Messiah at the town well. Worship that day was held in the place where townspeople came for water and social gossip. The focus that day was on the person of Jesus Christ, the foretold Messiah. Just imagine what that must have been like. Also imagine the disciples as they experienced that unique worship service, held outdoors, with no Jewish priest offering an animal sacrifice. A woman transformed from a life of shame into a joyful worshiper bore witness to the power of the Holy Spirit. She invited the townspeople to meet the Messiah and worship Father God with her.

Like the woman at the well with her spiritual traditions, you are comfortable with what is familiar. Like the woman at the well, you may assume your church and style of worship is the right one. Listen to Jesus' words, "true worship of the Father is done from spirit and truth." As you think about worship, be mindful without judgment. Notice how the words, melodies, and styles from any era can be a valid means of expressing worship when it comes from the heart and is done in a manner consistent with the Father's desire. There is no right place or right style by which to worship. What is right is that we worship God and do so in spirit and truth. Experience mindful worship with me as you read the lyrics from two different centuries. Journal the similarities and differences in your experience.

✐ *Journal Time—Exploring Worship from Different Eras*
Meditate on the lyrics of these hymns written 180 years apart:

"My Hope Is Built on Nothing Less" by Edward Mote and William Bradbury, 1834.[24]

"In Christ Alone, My Hope Is Found" by Stuart Townend and Keith Getty, 2001.[25]

What Scriptural themes are found in common? What are different?
Are the theme passages familiar to you?
What different emotions and images does each hymn evoke?

How might each impact worship in your faith community?

Is there any theological problem that you see with either set of lyrics?

How does repetition of phrases affect your worship?

If you can find an audio version of each, how does the music promote worship? Is there anything that detracts from worship?

✍ *Journal Time Ends—Exploring Worship from Different Eras*

Our Core Being Exists to Express Corporate Worship

> The Spirit is God's guarantee that he will give us the inheritance he promised when he purchased us to be his own people. He did this so we would praise and glorify him. (Ephesians 1:14 NLT)

My hope is that you realize the importance of meditative worship not merely as a solitary exercise but also as a shared corporate experience. I encourage you to read the lyrics of the following hymn in the presence of at least two other people and share with each other how these lyrics drew you to worship as a group. Remember that as few as two or three people guarantees God's presence.

> "I also tell you this: If two of you agree here on earth concerning anything you ask, my Father in heaven will do it for you. For where two or three gather together as my followers, I am there among them." (Matthew 18:19-20 NLT)

When you are mindful in meditation, you are, in your Core self, intentionally present in the moment. Christians who express intentional corporate worship can experience rich worship. When you express shared worship, it becomes a deeply meaningful moment with God. Our Core self expressing worship through our Relational being becomes orchestral. Each participant in corporate worship is one instrument of the orchestra, one voice in the choir that is praising the Creator. When I have led corporate worship in front of a congregation, it was a special privilege. I could hear the voices in unique harmony. I could see expressive faces radiating praise.

✍ *Journal Time—Experiencing Corporate Worship*
Look on the Internet for the following Hymn:

"We Have Seen God's Glory" by Gary Driskell and Mike Hudson, performed by Steve Green, 1986[26]

These lyrics touch me deeply each time I read them. The words give us a moment, right now, to share the awe of God's glory, Jesus Christ. Since we know Him in a personal, intimate way we have no other response than worshipful awe. The corporate witness of the twelve apostles who testified of God's glory after His resurrection is now our opportunity to experience and express regarding the amazing work of Jehovah God through the person of His Son. We can share the same message that is just as current and relevant today. You and I walk with Christ the King present in our lives. I look at you and you at me; we share the same knowledge. We share the same vista, the same awe, for the same Creator.

When reading the lyrics of this song with one another, follow the guidelines we have learned for creating a mindful experience: pay attention, in the moment, on purpose, without judgment. Journal the reflections of your small group on these lyrics.

Read the first stanza consisting of 12 lines, pausing at the end of each line intentionally using the psalmist's device to create mindfulness—Selah.

Notice how the lyrics describe the apostles. Observe what they are doing, thinking, and feeling. Notice how they act and the outcome of their actions. Identify with them as if you are with them two thousand plus years ago. Share your thoughts as a small group and record your corporate observations.

Read the second stanza again practicing Selah after each line. Note how the experience of the witnesses is how we give worshipful testimony. We are the vessels being used by God to share His Good News.

Notice how we are part of something greater. God is reaching out to those in need through us as we share the message of Christ and worship Jehovah. Journal your small group's reflections on being participants in God's Glory.

<u>Read the refrain</u> line by line including the repetitions and pause to reflect at the end of each. Share within your group the various positive thoughts, feelings, desires, and beliefs that are provoked by meditating on the lyrics in this time of worship.

This hymn is experiential in nature. It reflects scriptural truth in a narrative format. There is no Biblical quote as such. Should that lack of a quoted scripture reference be reason to not use this in worship?

What other observations came from your time of corporate worship?

✍ *Journal Time Ends—Experiencing Corporate Worship*

Coming to Awe, Finding Identity

I hope that this book has brought you to recognize who you are as a person and how much Jehovah God, your Creator, loves you. Each of the narrative chapters has aimed to teach you by a Scriptural character about how Core expressions of service and worship appear. Each apologetic chapter has aimed to expand your knowledge of science and Scripture in relation to consciousness as related to service and worship. In addition, each application chapter has aimed to help you personally experience and apply the concepts in a practical manner.

You, as a human being, have been formed in the image of Jehovah, our Creator, who from His Core Being has desired a deep personal relationship with you. As you recognize that you exist in His image, you are empowered to experience life in a new way, no longer focused on living for relationships, adapting to what pleases others or living to make others conform to what you expect them to be to meet your self-serving interests.

Conformity to the world is easier in the short run and following the voice of others can drown out the voice of Jehovah that our Core being strives to hear. It is not until we listen from our Core that we exist free of shame. We can find ourselves trapped in a pattern of reward and pleasure, experiencing what is pleasant for the moment, but then miss out on experiencing the richness of the awe encounter that comes from walking with God.

To experience, like Moses, a shedding of well-practiced personas and to live instead as the person whom God intended us to be is to find true joy. Like Moses, when we experience the amazing relationship that is possible with Jehovah God in His Core being we find fulfillment in our Core being by expressing our Core identity through those core gifts and traits uniquely endowed by Jehovah God. He relates to us as our Father who has loved us enough to send His Son for us. The Son reflected Jehovah God through His willing sacrifice so that you and I could be reconciled with the Father who expects us to be as holy as He is. The Spirit seals us to assure us that we are the children of a Holy God because of the work of Christ the Son.

Like David, you and I have the assurance through Christ that if we sin, when we own our sin by honest confession we find restoration and hear Jesus Christ assure us that we are forgiven and cleansed. It is He, our Advocate, who pleads our case before the Righteous Judge. He, Jesus Christ, our High Priest is sitting in a place of mercy. I can approach that place boldly because in My Core existence I find in Him one who has identified with and has experienced our humanity, while remaining sinless. There at that mercy seat, you and I find help in time of need.

The example that Paul shared of Christ's demonstration of service displayed in His life, demonstrates that it is possible to live in this world and not conform to it. By His example of service that glorifies the Father and is the expression of Jehovah God in His Core being, we are challenged to follow His example. The transformation required could only occur from a Core mindset within a person who desires to serve God.

And now, in this final chapter, we have learned that the ultimate expression of our Core being culminates in worship. To praise Jehovah God for His majesty, to praise the Father for His Holiness, to praise the Son for His redemption, to praise the Spirit for His ministry is to begin to grasp what we owe to Him for who He is. To worship Him as Lord is to be caught up in the greatest moment of awe.

Chapter 8

REFLECTIONS AND AFTERTHOUGHTS

The Search for Identity

Wil Anderson asked me what my plan and structure was for the subject matter when I began the journey to write this series. "Wil, it has been on my mind and in my heart for a long time. I just need to get it out on paper." I encouraged him to wait as I began writing. His experience of authoring publications was to define the desired audience and then to define the objectives. Next, I asked myself how this manuscript compared to what was already published; what would be unique about this material? Like the tagline of Star Trek, I set out to boldly go where I believed no one had gone before. The scientific material I planned to share to support my apologetic argument of scripture was based on recent neurocognitive science. I did not find comparative literature in Christian publications. I am sure others will write on these concepts in the future. My prayer is that God will use this series to stir your heart.

The content of the *Coming to Awe, Finding Identity* series has the potential to reach four audiences. The primary audience is for small group ministry in faith communities. Each of the three books may be used in a six to nine week small group study. The participants will find the material helpful in building maturity among believers.

The second audience is anyone who desires an in-depth study of apologetics, the study of how science and scripture can be in harmony. The three books are progressively deeper in content to emphasize our Creator's intention shown in His handiwork. The scientific material is a key source in the discovery of awe. The latest neuro-cognitive findings strengthen the evidence of an intentional Creator who designed the human mind with amazing capabilities for healing and growth.

The third audience is for recovery programs within faith communities. The church has become a resource for hurting people who struggle with hurts, habits, addictions, and woundedness. The principles in the *Coming to Awe, Finding Identity* series address the spiritual truth needed to counter the lies that the Relational self believes. The scientific findings show the importance of limbic calming and the means consistent with scripture to allow neurological changes that one may live in truth from his or her Core self.

The final audience is the adult who likes to scan new material for fresh ideas. Some readers have reported meaningful gems that enriched their lives. Some reported a greater respect and appreciation for spouse, family members, and fellow believers. Others found their hearts stirred to a deeper relationship with Christ; others witnessed how these individuals expressed service and worship.

Existence Began with the Creator's Breath

Let everything that breathes sing praises to the Lord! Praise the Lord! (Psalm 150:6 NLT)

Core identity was a phrase that emerged through the years as these concepts became incorporated into my philosophy and practice of counseling. Core self and Core being became synonyms for the concept. You have learned that these terms represent the unique identity that our Creator gives to each human being from conception. Existence is undeniable. Our existence is a reality from birth; thus each of us has a unique Core identity. Our Core self goes on in life and moves beyond the events that shape us.

Each breath, whether conscious or unconscious, is evidence of the existence of our Core being. To help you understand more about your Core identity, you provided five positive adjectives that you would use to describe yourself. We used the phenomenology of William James who defined self as the subject of life. The adjectives are our personal descriptions of how we view and value life. Our Core identity continues from one moment to the next always learning and experiencing. Energy, meaning, and hope come from our Core being. The desire for a relationship with our Creator also comes from our Core being.

The Rosetta stone of identity is when awe captures our attention. Our Core being is brought to such a moment when our senses experience that we are a part of something that is larger than we realize. The beauty of creation witnessed at the moment of awe absorbs our attention. Standing amazed, in speechless wonder, or mouth agape are such inadequate descriptions of an encounter with awe. Our existence can seem insignificant in relation to the grandeur; nevertheless we know we are. We realize at that moment that we are not alone; our Supreme Creator is behind the scenes of what we just witnessed. Awe confirms our existence, our identity, and our Creator who loves us.

Experience Can Alter Identity

After nine months of solitude, we are born and emerge into the social world with our Core identity present and in the moment. The womb no longer softens the sensory world. Bright lights, loud noises, cold air, and the lack of embracing tissue are a stark reality for the infant. Other human beings interact with and expect a response from the infant. The Core self eventually learns to tolerate the environment and begins to acquire knowledge that promotes intellectual and behavioral growth.

Core identity soon recognizes others exist who are not "I." These others expect certain responses; when the infant complies, he or she is shown pleasure and approval. This is when socialization and behavioral shaping by the child's social circles begins. If Core self does not comply, the consequence may be displeasure or pain. As disapproval becomes the pattern, the mind creates a Relational identity to show to others what they want to see. The Relational self has the job to protect and preserve Core identity from shame and pain. The Relational self fulfills the Core identity's needs, wishes, wants, and desires. The expectations of others tend to define the child's Relational identity possibly preventing Core identity from becoming executive in life.

When the Relational self is present to assure acceptance, approval, or control, the child has lost consciousness of Core Self. The Core self is still there but to avoid pain and shame may stay in the background. Such experiences shape people as adults to wear a mask or to create a persona. Though the Core desire may lead to a conversion to Christ, the Relational self may remain bound by past shame.

Identification Restores Core Identity
When I discovered your words, I devoured them.

They are my joy and my heart's delight, for I bear your name,
O Lord God of Heaven's Armies. (Jeremiah 15:16 NLT)

As the person grows in his or her relationship with Christ, a renewing of the mind takes place. That transformation through faith in Christ allows the Core self to once again exert autonomy and live life to honor God rather than merely to comply with others. Like the Christians in Galatia, Core self finds itself free from the bondage of the Law and basking in the sunlight of Grace. One major truth that provides freedom is that Core self hears the message of reconciliation through Christ. Jesus Christ, the Creator took on flesh to live, to die, and to be raised again that we may live free of guilt and shame. His death and shed blood makes us pure in the sight of Holy God. All our sin is atoned. All our debt is paid.

By the death and resurrection of Jesus Christ, we are made heirs. Through the work of Christ, we become the children of God, Jew and Gentile alike. When we accept Him as our Lord and Savior, we are called by His name. Our heritage is heavenly based, not earthly based. James, the Apostle spoke this truth that Luke recorded. He declared that God's chosen were any who claimed the work of Christ and identified with Him.

Afterward I will return and restore the fallen house of David. I will rebuild its ruins and restore it, so that the rest of humanity might seek the Lord, including the Gentiles—all those I have called to be mine. The Lord has spoken (Acts 15:17 NLT)

How incredible it is that the Creator took on human form and by His life, death, burial, and resurrection reconciled you and me to our Creator.

Relationships Can Free the Core Self

So take a new grip with your tired hands and strengthen your weak knees. Mark out a straight path for your feet so that those who are weak and lame will not fall but become strong. (Hebrews 12:13-14 NLT)

The believer can know the truth of the cleansing work of Christ in his life but continue to live from the Relational self. The reason has to do with the issue of shame. When the Relational self is formed in early childhood, shame is the mechanism that strengthens it. When others say we are bad or wrong, we believe that there is an inherent flaw in us that cannot change. That shame becomes the motivation to hide our Core self based on that mistaken belief. In our Core identity, we have a sense of right and wrong in terms of moral choice. That knowledge is used by Core self to choose to do what is right. However, the belief that we are wrong by the nature of who we are leaves us irredeemable.

Jesus Christ never did one act or had one thought of sin. That was necessary to cleanse our guilt over our sinful choices. The death of Christ also addressed the problem of shame. Scripture shows that the Creator's plan involved choosing the right moment in human history when human culture was using the most humiliating means of punishment. Death by hanging had long been seen as a curse. The proverb was common knowledge: "Cursed is anyone who is hanged from a tree." Criminals were determined irredeemable and death was the only solution for society's sake. The Romans thought that the public display of criminals on a cross along public thoroughfares would be a deterrent. The placard above their heads listed their crimes against society. Passersby would shout at them and further humiliate them as they hung there dying. Jesus Christ was subjected to that death of shame. Hanging in public view, His placard of crimes read, "This is Jesus, King of the Jews." Jesus Christ, became shame for us. He became hope for the shameful.

Through Jesus, we are redeemable in spite of what any others might say. Two Psalms express the freedom and protection the Lord provides His own from shame.

O Lord, I give my life to you. I trust in you, my God! Do not let me be disgraced, or let my enemies rejoice in my defeat. No one who trusts in you will ever be disgraced... (Psalm 25:1-3 NLT)

Those who look to him for help will be radiant with joy; no shadow of shame will darken their faces. (Psalm 34:5 NLT)

The relationship with Jesus Christ transforms our character and frees us from shame. A faith community or fellowship of believers also helps to release us from shame. When we share our hurts, habits, and hang ups, we allow others to help us recognize the lies from our past. Accountability to other believers is a powerful tool in breaking the bondage that shame creates. Strengthening one another's faith builds stamina and resilience. Paul encouraged believers to challenge one another lovingly to stand strong and firm in faith supporting one another as we anticipate Christ's return.

Let us hold tightly without wavering to the hope we affirm, for God can be trusted to keep his promise. Let us think of ways to motivate one another to acts of love and good works. (Hebrews 10:23-25 NLT)

Each believer is encouraged to live from his or her Core identity. No matter our condition, tiredness and woundedness need a change of pace, a new grip, and level ground to walk on to build up stamina and promote healing. The broken mind and wounded spirit is in need of the ministration of the Great Physician who came to bring healing by His stripes.

Expression Refreshes the Soul

But it is no shame to suffer for being a Christian. <u>Praise God for the privilege of being called by his name</u>! (1 Peter 4:16 NLT)

The Lord is my shepherd; I have all that I need. He lets me rest in green meadows; he leads me beside peaceful streams. <u>He renews my strength</u>. He guides me along right paths, bringing honor to his name. (Psalm 23:1-3 NLT)

Service and worship were the focus of this third book in the *Coming to Awe, Finding Identity* series. These expressions come naturally from our Core being as we revel in what our Creator has accomplished for us. Science has demonstrated that people who are grateful are happier and healthier. Those who live as mindfully as possible from their Core being can attest to that as their experience. Those who live expressing divine purpose from their Core identity are able to show love and grace to others. Serving others from our Core identity honors our Creator and bears witness to the power of God manifest in our life.

Worship is the ultimate expression of Core self giving praise and glory to the Creator. We worship Him for His creation, for His incarnation, for His redemption, for His forgiveness, and for His prepared dwelling place where we will live with Him eternally. A worshiping believer encounters awe embodied in His majesty. Scripture is filled with reasons to praise Him. As His children, we can never run short of praise.

Through service and worship our Core being is refreshed. The time we spend with Him can reflect in our Core identity. Oh, that others might see His glory in our countenance. May we live so that others will want to know the Savior! May we live so fellow believers are encouraged and challenged to live from their Core to the glory of the Creator!

I thank you for sharing this journey with me. I pray that you will grow into a closer relationship to glorify our Creator.

A Final Request

Please go to http://lowellroutley.com/survey and answer a brief evaluation survey of how these books have impacted you. This survey will ask you to provide your email address. For your security, your information will not be shared with anyone. Your email address will not be given or sold to anyone. I as the author will be the only one with access to the information you provide. Your comments will be read and incorporated in future publications. You may opt out of this list at any time.

BIBLIOGRAPHY

[The following books were the resources used throughout this series to develop a consistent scientific and theological basis for the apologetic arguments.]

Abernethy, Alexis D. Worship That Changes Lives: Multidisciplinary and Congregational Perspectives on Spiritual Transformation. Grand Rapids, Mich.: Baker Academic, 2008. Print.

Baars, Bernard J. *A Cognitive Theory of Consciousness*. Cambridge, England: Cambridge UP, 1988. Print.

Baars, Bernard J. In the Theater of Consciousness: The Workspace of the Mind. New York: Oxford UP, 1997. Print.

Berkhof, Louis, and Louis Berkhof. *Systematic Theology*. New ed. Grand Rapids, Mich.: W.B. Eerdmans Pub., 1996. Print.

Bruce, F. F. The Epistles to the Colossians, to Philemon, and to the Ephesians. Grand Rapids, Mich.: W.B. Eerdmans, 1984. Print.

Churchland, Paul M. The Engine of Reason, the Seat of the Soul: A Philosophical Journey into the Brain. Cambridge, Mass.: MIT, 1995. Print.

Crick, Francis. The Astonishing Hypothesis: The Scientific Search for the Soul. New York: Scribner, 1994. Print.

Damasio, Antonio R. Descartes' Error: Emotion, Reason, and the Human Brain. New York: Putnam, 1994. Print.

Damasio, Antonio R. *Looking for Spinoza: Joy, Sorrow, and the Feeling Brain*. Orlando, Fla.: Harcourt, 2003. Print.

Damasio, Antonio R. The Feeling of What Happens: Body and Emotion in the Making of Consciousness. New York: Harcourt Brace, 1999. Print.

Darley, John M., and C. Daniel Batson. ""From Jerusalem to Jericho": A Study of Situational and Dispositional Variables in Helping Behavior." *Journal of Personality and Social Psychology* 27.1 (1973): 101-08. Print.

Edersheim, Alfred. *Sketches of Jewish Social Life*. Updated ed. Peabody, Mass.: Hendrickson, 1994. Print.

Einstein, Albert. *Living Philosophies*. New York: Simon and Schuster, 1931. Print.

Erikson, Erik H. *The Life Cycle Completed: A Review*. New York: Norton, 1982. Print.

Falk, Geoffrey D. The Science of the Soul: On Consciousness and the Structure of Reality. Nevada City, CA: Blue Dolphin Pub., 2004. Print.

Fee, Gordon D. *The First Epistle to the Corinthians*. Grand Rapids, Mich.: W.B. Eerdmans Pub., 1987. Print.

Hamilton, Victor P. *The Book of Genesis*. Grand Rapids, Mich.: Wm. B. Eerdmans Pub., 1995. Print.

Holy Bible: New Living Translation. Wheaton, Ill.: Tyndale House, 1996. Print.

James, William. *The Principles of Psychology*. Authorized ed. New York: Dover Publications, 1950. Print.

Josephus, Flavius, and William Whiston. *The Works of Josephus: Complete and Unabridged*. New Updated ed. Peabody, Mass.: Hendrickson, 1987. Print.

Keil, Carl Friedrich, and Franz Delitzsch. *Commentary on the Old Testament*, Mass.: Hendrickson, 2006. Print.

Maddi, Salvatore R. *Personality Theories: A Comparative Analysis*. Rev. ed. Homewood, Ill.: Dorsey, 1972. Print.

Moo, Douglas J. *The Epistle to the Romans*. Grand Rapids, Mich.: W.B. Eerdmans Pub., 1996. Print.

Nelson's Complete Book of Bible Maps & Charts: Old and New Testaments. Rev. and Updated ed. Nashville, Tenn.: Thomas Nelson, 1996. Print.

Newberg, Andrew B., and Mark Robert Waldman. *How God Changes Your Brain: Breakthrough Findings from a Leading Neuroscientist*. New York: Ballantine, 2009. Print.

Newberg, Andrew B. *Principles of Neurotheology*. Farnham, Surrey, England: Ashgate Pub, 2010. Print.

Newberg, Andrew B., Eugene G. Aquili, and Vince Rause. *Why God won't go away: brain science and the biology of belief*. New York: Ballantine Books, 2001. Print.

Oswalt, John N. *The Book of Isaiah*. Grand Rapids, MI: Eerdmans, 1998. Print.

Pfeiffer, Charles F. *Baker's Bible Atlas*. Grand Rapids: Baker Book House, 2003. Print.

Polhill, John B. *Paul and His Letters*. Nashville, TN: Broadman & Holman, 1999. Print.

Skinner, B. F. *Beyond Freedom and Dignity*. New York: Knopf, 1971. Print.

Skinner, B. F. *Walden Two*. New York: Macmillan, 1976. Print.

Vine, W. E., and Merrill F. Unger. *Vine's Complete Expository Dictionary of Old and New Testament Words*: With Topical Index. Nashville: T. Nelson, 1996. Print.

Zinn, Jon. Wherever You Go, There You Are: Mindfulness Meditation in Everyday Life. New York: Hyperion, 1994. Print.

END NOTES

Chapter 1

1 Geisel, Theodore. *Happy Birthday to You!* New York: Random House Children's Books, 1959. Print.

2 "adjective." *Collins English Dictionary—Complete & Unabridged 10th Edition.* HarperCollins Publishers. 13 Jan. 2015. Dictionary.com <http://dictionary.reference.com/browse/adjective>.

3 James, William. *The Principles of Psychology.* Authorized ed. New York: Dover Publications, 1950. Print.

Chapter 2

4 Maimonides, Moses, and Eliyahu Touger. *Mishneh Torah.* New York ; Jerusalem: Moznaim Pub., 1986. Print.

5 Chrysler, Rabbi Eliezer. "Must One Teach a Trade to His Son?" *Outlines Of Halachos—Kidushin 82.* Kollel Iyun Hadaf, 4 June 2011. Web. 13 Jan. 2015. <http://www.dafyomi.co.il/kidushin/halachah/kd-hl-082.htm>.

6 "The Septuagint." *BibliaHebraica.org, A Research Site Providing Resources for Biblical Study.* Jan. 2003. Web. 13 Jan. 2015. <http://www.bibliahebraica.com/the_texts/septuagint.htm>.

Chapter 3

7 Darley, John M., and C. Daniel Batson. ""From Jerusalem to Jericho": A Study of Situational and Dispositional Variables in Helping Behavior." *Journal of Personality and Social Psychology* 27.1 (1973): 101-08. Print.

[8] Batson, C. Daniel, Nadia Ahmad, and Jo-Ann Tsang. "Four Motives For Community Involvement." *Journal of Social Issues* 58.1 (2002): 429-45. Print.

[9] Myers, Isabel Briggs, and Peter B. Myers. *Gifts Differing: Understanding Personality Type*. Palo Alto, Calif.: Davies-Black Pub., 1995. Print.

Chapter 4

[10] Friesen, Garry, and J. Robin Maxson. *Decision Making & the Will of God: A Biblical Alternative to the Traditional View*. Portland, OR: Multnomah, 1980. Print.

[11] "Chariots in Red Sea: 'Irrefutable Evidence'." *WND*. World Net Daily, 1 June 2012. Web. 13 Jan. 2015. <http://www.wnd.com/2012/06/chariots-in-red-sea-irrefutable-evidence/>.

Section 3.3

[12] "Fyodor Dostoevsky." BrainyQuote.com. Xplore Inc, 2015. Web. 19 January 2015. <http://www.brainyquote.com/quotes/quotes/f/fyodordost402782.html>

[13] "Great Quotes on Worship." *Experiencing Worship*. EXW, 24 Sept. 2013. Web. 20 Jan. 2015. <http://www.experiencingworship.com/worship-articles/general/2001-7-Great-Quotes-on-p2.html>.

Chapter 6

[14] "hermeneutics." *Random House Kernerman Webster's College Dictionary*. 2010. K Dictionaries Ltd. Copyright 2005, 1997, 1991. by Random House, Inc. Web 16 Jan. 2015 <http://www.thefreedictionary.com/hermeneutics>

[15] Ken, Thomas. "Doxology." *CyberHymnal.org*. Net Hymnal. 1674. Web. 21 Jan. 2015. <http://cyberhymnal.org/htm/p/r/praisegf.htm>.

[16] Egermeier, Elsie E. *Egermeier's Bible Story Book*. Anderson, Ind: Warner, 1955. Print.

[17] Piaget, Jean. *Genetic Epistemology*. New York: Columbia UP, 1970. Print.

Chapter 7
<u>Print out the lyrics at the following links for use in this application
chapter on worship.</u>

[18] Darby, J. N. *Hymns and Spiritual Songs for the Little Flock*. New
York, USA: Loizeaux Brothers, Bible Truth Depot. 1881.

[19] Watts, Isaac. *Not all the blood of beasts*. (1707) Hymns and Spiritual Songs. New York, USA: Loizeaux Brothers, Bible Truth Depot.
1881. Web. 21 January 2015. **<http://www.stempublishing.com/
hymns/ss/43>**

[20] Dark, Elizabeth. *Through Thy precious body broken inside the veil*.
The Vestry Hymn and Tune Book, edited by Adoniram J. Gordon.
Boston, Massachusetts: Henry A. Young & Company, 1872. Web.
21 January 2015. **<http://www.hymntime.com/tch/htm/i/n/s/
insidetv.htm>**

[21] Medley, Samuel. *Come, let us sing the matchless worth*. (1790)
New York, USA: Loizeaux Brothers, Bible Truth Depot. 1881. Web.
21 January 2015 **<http://www.stempublishing.com/hymns/ss/196>**

[22] Watts, Isaac. *Alas and Did My Savior Bleed*. (1709) Hymns and
Spiritual Songs. New York, USA: Loizeaux Brothers, Bible Truth
Depot. 1881. Web. 21 January 2015. **<http://library.timelesstruths.
org/music/At_the_Cross_Hudson>**

[23] Bevan, Frances. *A thousand, a thousand thanksgivings*. (1858) Hymns
of Truth and Praise. Port Colborne, ON: Gospel Folio Press. 2011.
Web. 21 January 2015. **<http://saintsserving.net/song.php?id=85>**

[24] Mote, Edward. William Bradbury. *My Hope Is Built on Nothing
Less*. (1834). The Believers Hymn Book. London: Pickering & Inglis,
LTD. 1881. Web. 21 January 2015. **<https://www.hymnal.net/en/
hymn/h/298>**

[25] Townend, Stuart. Keith Getty. *In Christ Alone, My Hope Is Found*.
Ireland: Thankyou Music. 2001. Web. 21 January 2015. **<http://www.
stuarttownend.co.uk/song/in-christ-alone/>**

[26] Driskell, Gary. Mike Hudson. *We Have Seen God's Glory*. USA:
Ariose Music. 1986. Performed by Steve Green. CD. Web. 21
January 2015. **<http://www.stevegreenministries.org/product/
we-have-seen-gods-glory/>**

CPSIA information can be obtained at www.ICGtesting.com
Printed in the USA
LVOW01s1035080815

449210LV00005B/66/P